Getting
Started
as a
Residential
Child Care
Worker?

Getting Started as a Residential Child Care Worker?

A GUIDE FOR BEGINNERS

Jesse E. Crone

CWLA Press
Arlington, VA

The Child Welfare League of America is the nation's oldest and largest membership-based child welfare organization. We are committed to engaging people everywhere in promoting the well-being of children, youth, and their families, and protecting every child from harm.

CHILD WELFARE LEAGUE OF AMERICA, INC.
HEADQUARTERS
2345 Crystal Drive, Suite 250, Arlington, VA 22202-4815
E-mail: books@cwla.org

CURRENT PRINTING (last digit)
10

Printed in the United States of America

ISBN # 978-0-87868-218-8

Library of Congress Cataloging-in-Publication Data
Crone, Jesse E.
    Getting started as a residential child care worker? : a guide for beginners /
    by Jesse E. Crone.
        xv, 143 p. ; 22 cm.
        ISBN # 978-0-87868-218-8 (pbk. : alk. paper)
        1. Child care workers—United States.
        2. Group homes for children—United States.
            HV863 .C76 1984
            362.7/32 19   83025197

Contents

Acknowledgments

The author received a great deal of help in preparing this volume. Unfortunately, it won't be possible to thank everyone who contributed. Special thanks, however, must go to virtually all 60 members of the Interstate Consortium on Residential Child Care, who gave us time during their meetings to speak with Mark Mercer on the topic of child care training.

Extensive research was carried out during the earlier stages of preparation, including a review of the literature on the topic. Many child care workers were interviewed, and many of the issues confronted here were explored in tape-recorded interviews or intensive discussions.

I also wish to thank the Glenmede Trust Company (Philadelphia) for a grant that helped make this book possible.

Introduction

Our goal here is to give a practical, down-to-earth presentation of child care work for inexperienced child care workers or for those persons who want to enter this challenging field. This volume, therefore, is not about child development. You can find any number of good books about how children change and develop as they grow. If you are familiar with any of the fields related to the study of human behavior, you are probably aware that we have a lot of information and a number of theories about what makes people tick.

We certainly think that you should know these theories, and we urge you to continue your education, but we want to let you know right away that you won't learn much about psychological theories or research from this book. You will find, however, the practical knowledge that is the foundation of good child care work. Children need to be adequately cared for and protected before supportive counseling makes any sense. You have to guard their health and safety. You have to make sure that they're clean, well-fed, and clothed. You have to work to maintain their surroundings as a warm, homelike place. You have to learn to manage their behavior in a tolerant, adult fashion, respecting their dignity as individuals. You have to learn how to watch and listen and how to think about what you see, and *that*, if you think about it, is something that most people don't do. Then, maybe, it's time to talk.

When you get down to the basics, a good child care worker is a good homemaker. Our society, unfortunately, doesn't place a lot of value on that. Seeing that there are napkins on the table and that the bathrooms are clean just doesn't stack up very well against, say, hang-gliding or brain surgery, but, well, there it is. Male child care workers have a particularly hard time with this end of their work. They have a tendency to let the women do it. This is all right as long as the women let them get away with it and, in this day and age, that usually isn't very long. In practice, a lot of tension between staff members results from adopting this perspective. Any old-timer will tell you that the big "conflicts of philosophy" that people sometimes get into are usually caused by trifling irritations like cleaning out the sink while somebody else is out playing catch with the kids. Big conflicts can be resolved. Little exasperations just mount up.

Another basic responsibility has to do with the health and safety of the children in your care; if you think about it, you are about to be given a very important trust. You will have what we call "life responsibility." You are responsible for the lives of the children in your charge.

Many of you have had a form of that responsibility before. Any experience that you have had of "life responsibility" will help you understand what we mean. If you have been a lifeguard, a camp counselor, a noncom in the military, or a parent, to mention just a few possibilities, you have a notion of what it means to assume total responsibility for the health and safety of others. These "others" now are children, and children have a mixture of carelessness and curiosity that makes accidents inevitable. You have to know *exactly* what to do in the event of an emergency.

Managing children's behavior is another basic. Children need firmness and consistency from the adults who deal with them. They also need tolerance and to be listened to. If you work with troubled children, it isn't always easy to keep from getting angry and frustrated. If you find out how to keep your temper all the time, please contact us immediately and we'll write another book. If you're a complete beginner, here's a little good advice: for the time being, keep your eyes, ears, and mind open and your mouth firmly set in a locked and closed position. Do not save the world this week or the next; you'll put everyone out of a job. If you've got a good sense of humor, so much the better, because you'll need it. You have taken on a complex and difficult job with a lot of pressures.

There's a good side to it, too. This work can be the most rewarding experience of your life. The main payoff is the kind of person you can become if you stick with it. You can't learn about other people without learning about yourself. By becoming a good child care worker you become a good person — strong, capable, honest, and loving. You learn how to truly listen to others and to deal with people in effective ways. You also learn to love this field and the wonderful people in it.

The fact that you've chosen this job probably says some good things about you. We want to take this opportunity to welcome you to the field. We hope that this book makes your life easier.

SO YOU WANT TO BE A CHILD CARE WORKER?

Why?

Before we talk about child care, let's take a good look at you. Why did you choose this job?

If you spend a few years interviewing people for child care positions, you begin to notice that people have all kinds of reasons for coming to the field, some good and, to be truthful, some bad.

One familiar applicant is the person who wants to save the world. This person is all fired up with idealism and wants to make things better for other people. Now, that's good as far as it goes. Most of us share that idealism, although our eyes get a little less wild every year. The thing is, can you stick it out? Saving the world is a long, hard job. The victories are won by hard work and there are plenty of defeats. And, you know, sometimes the world just doesn't want to be saved.

You have to make sure that the expectations you place on the children are realistic. The idealist sometimes expects too much and is therefore disappointed. After a week or so, he or she looks at you and says, "I've been working on these kids all week and they haven't gotten any better."

Some people enjoy working with people. They like the idea of being paid just to relate with other human beings, rather than selling things or pushing buttons. That's okay, too, but it does take a lot of work to make a good child care worker.

Some people like exercising authority. That can be fine, too, if the person isn't terribly rigid. At some point or other, some kid is going to tell you in words of one syllable what you can do with your rules. What will you do then?

Some misguided souls think that it's a very easy job. All you have to do is watch some kids, right? Wrong.

Low expectations are as bad as high expectations. Workers who don't expect *anything* from the children either become like children themselves and a problem for staff, or they stand by fiddling while Rome burns. You've got to have something of your own inside you that you want to communicate to the children—call it what you will —values, standards, ethics, morals, or maybe just love. What's inside you? What do you want from other people? Who are you? Why are you here?

Are you the kind of person who can let other people lean on you or are you just looking for someone to lean on? In this work, the children do the leaning. Can you handle that?

How well do you take verbal abuse? Can you control feelings? Do you have a bad temper?

Is it difficult for you to tell others what to do? Or

do you like ordering people around? How do you react in a crisis?

You're the only person who can answer these questions. Take a good, long look at yourself. Make sure that this is what you want to do.

We are now going to give you a closely guarded trade secret. It doesn't sound like much of an answer but it's a good beginning. *People who love children generally make good child care workers, if they work at it.*

One more thing. Sometime very soon you will probably find yourself doubting that you made the right decision. Someday you will come home dirty and tired and be unable to remember the last time one of the kids said something nice to you. You might also feel useless and think that no one understands what you have to contend with. Well, just remember this: *doubt is a healthy sign; it shows that you are alive and asking questions.*

WHAT IS CHILD CARE WORK?

This is the warning on the label: your responsibilities as a child care worker will depend very much on the agency that employs you. There are several generalizations that we can make but basically it's up to you to find out exactly what your employer expects.

Child care is, first of all, a job. For some reason, people in the field sometimes choose to ignore this. You are hired by your employer to perform a series of duties. Make sure that you know what they are.

The approach that your agency takes will depend on a number of factors. The main one will be the type of children accepted by your agency and what it is trying to do with them. Here we discuss what all child care workers have in common.

All child care workers have "life responsibility," as we have said earlier. You are responsible for protecting the health and safety of your children. You will note that we say "your children." Within a week you will too; if you don't, it's probably a bad sign. Beyond this, you have a basic responsibility to react to any dangers to the health and safety of *any* children in the care of your agency, even if they are not "your children." You cannot, for instance, fail to break up a fight just because the children involved are not your immediate responsibility. So, at some fundamental level, you are a lifeguard. You have to keep your eyes open for dangerous or unhealthy conditions. These are discussed in detail in chapter 3.

You might call child care work "parenting." As a professional child care worker, however, you must always remember that "your" children already have parents. You should not try to replace them. Don't give the child the impression that you will always be there to help. You won't. Your relationship with the child, however positive, is time-limited.

Although the techniques used to manage children differ from agency to agency, and you must know what your agency accepts and approves as a response to children's behavior, one thing is certain. You cannot teach a child anything by hurting or humiliating him or her. Any hurtful or unnecessary use of force can result in your losing your job.

You will find that most children will respond to an adult who is fair and consistent. If you make what you want very clear at all times, you won't have much trouble. If you are hesitant, unsure, or inconsistent, you will have a great deal of trouble.

If you are really in control of the situation, you don't often have to display your control. You can afford, for instance, to allow the children to be angry with you and to express their anger openly. Experience tells us that the more "control statements," "do this," "don't do that," made by a worker, the less his or her actual control of the situation. A good worker makes sure that each child is aware of ways to get the worker's attention that don't involve misbehavior.

When you have mastered these skills, you can start sharpening up your "observational skills" — the skills involved in observing and analyzing a child's or a group's behavior. Don't expect to become an expert immediately. You will have enough to do for a while just handling the basics.

And, of course, your analyses and observations aren't worth very much unless you can communicate them to others both in speech and writing. These important skills are, unfortunately, often ignored.

A good worker has to be adept at "programming"—thinking up and planning activities. A good "programmer" is literally worth his or her weight in gold to the agency.

Crisis management is a specialized form of training in handling difficult situations. We discuss it in this book because it is an important item in any worker's kitbag. Crisis management includes how to talk a kid down when he or she is about to explode, and ways of handling physical confrontations without hurting anyone or getting hurt.

Every worker has to be a good team player. You have to learn how to work with other professionals.

Finally, "supportive counseling"—talking to kids in a way that helps them grow—is, of course, probably the reason why you took the job in the first place. It's well worth it.

Well, that, briefly, completes the list of common responsibilities and necessary skills. You will find them all elaborated upon as you read further.

1
The Big Picture

This is not a history of child care, or, for that matter, of child care group care settings. A history would be long and wouldn't be of much use to you now. You may ask why we are bothering to include any history at all. We do because we don't think that you can understand modern attitudes toward children, families, and child care organizations unless you know something about how these attitudes came to be.

WHAT IS A CHILD?

It may interest you to know that the concept of "childhood" is relatively new, historically speaking. In the Middle Ages there was really no such thing as a "child." Children were generally regarded as household pets until they arrived at the young (according to our standards) age when they were expected to begin assuming the responsibilities of an adult.

Medieval people were not particularly affectior ate toward their children. Since many children died before reaching adulthood, their attitude may just have been a way of protecting themselves against loss.

When we say "child," we generally mean someone who is too young to accept responsibility for his or her actions. But in the Middle Ages it was not uncommon for very young children to be executed for theft or other crimes. In fact, if you were old enough to commit a crime, you were considered old enough to be punished for it. Such practices continued well into the 1800s.

Until recently, a person with authority over a child could get away with just about anything short of murder. Laws protecting children from adults date from the second half of the 1800s. As a matter of fact, laws preventing cruelty to animals were generally in place before cruelty-to-children laws. Some of the first prosecutions for child cruelty were under animal cruelty laws.

Our concept of what a child is has changed a great deal during the twentieth century, some of the most important changes occurring in the past few years. State laws defining what a "child," "juvenile," or "minor" is also have changed enormously in the last twenty years. Of course, laws have always varied from state to state and they still do.

In the past, the cut-off point for the age at which society considered someone a child was generally somewhere between fourteen and sixteen years of age. Anyone older was thought to be an adult, both by the courts and society-in-general. Practically speaking, however, it was also usually true that a person was not accorded the full rights of an adult until age twenty-one, "the age of majority." Over the past twenty years the trend has been to raise the age for the reduced responsibilities of childhood while lowering the age for the increased rights of adulthood. For example, we have extended the right to vote and make contracts to younger people at the same time that we have made laws that generally consider a person under eighteen to be less than fully responsible for his or her actions.

The law increasingly has become concerned with the legal rights of children. Even ten years ago, the attitude of juvenile courts was "paternalistic"—judges assumed sweeping authority to decide the best thing for the child. In practice this meant that a child might be put in an institution, labeled a "juvenile delinquent," or subjected to a variety of other drastic forms of treatment without anyone being required to prove much of anything. In most jurisdictions a child's parents could simply come into court and swear that the child was "incorrigible" or "unmanageable" and the child could be placed in an institution, usually an institution for offenders. This cannot happen any more. The trend is toward giving children some of the same legal rights that adults have. You may have heard recently of cases in which juveniles have initiated court cases, occasionally against their parents. This would have been unthinkable ten years ago.

There are still differences, of course, in the manner in which the law approaches children and the manner in which it approaches adults. There are, for example, the so-called "status offenses," like truancy. Obviously, not going to school is illegal for a child but not for an adult. There is, as well, a continuing concern for the protection of children, particularly abused, neglected, or abandoned children. These are not likely to change.

WHAT IS A FAMILY?

The word "family" is one of those common words that really don't have a precise definition. Modern lifestyles have made it increasingly difficult to decide what a family is. Our concept of family has changed as drastically as our concept of child. Originally, a family was a large network of related persons; it included aunts, uncles, cousins, and sometimes even more distantly related people. The core of a family was a mother and a father living together and caring for children.

This pattern is age-old. Generally speaking, our ancestors lived out their lives in the presence of this large support group. In times of trouble, help would usually come from other family members. Despite the enormous differences among family groupings across different cultural and ethnic groups, the extended family occupied an especially important place in the lives of Americans until recent times.

At present, many children have little or no contact with their extended families. Many have never met uncles, aunts, and cousins, and seldom see grandparents, who may live in other areas of the country. This is part of the price Americans have paid for mobility. Recent figures show that one out of every four Americans moves at least once in a period of twelve months.

High divorce rates and changes in basic social mores have created a great many single-parent families. For an increasing number of children, family life has a totally new meaning. For instance, lack of support from extended family and the realities of life as a single parent supporting a family mean more dependence on schools, public agencies, and professional child care agencies for the process of rearing children. Grandma isn't there to take the kids during the day so the kids go to the day care center.

There is considerable controversy in this country over whether the growing roles of schools and social agencies are desirable. Many feel that the state is stripping away the family's traditional power and, indeed, has caused most of the problems facing the family. In fact, however, schools and social agencies are merely reacting to rapid social events that have already occurred and are attempting to fill the gaps left by widespread changes in American family life. One thing is certain: there are no simple solutions to these problems.

THE HISTORY OF AMERICAN CHILD CARE INSTITUTIONS

The history of child care institutions generally dates from the mid-1800s. Most of the older institutions still in existence in the United States were established just after the Civil War. During this period, people were beginning to face the problems associated with living in large industrial cities. An increasing number were coming to the cities and working long hours in factories. Living conditions for the urban poor were extremely difficult. As an example of a child care solution offered to remedy a problem of those times, the charter of one child care institution, founded in 1867, said that it provided "shelter and a moral example for children of drunken or dissolute parents." When discussing early institutions, it is easy to lose sight of the fact that they were better than nothing. Previously, children were simply left to starve in the streets. The frequently harsh conditions in early institutions should be seen in this light.

Another practice was to send children out to work for tradesmen, farmers, or factory owners. As you can imagine, many of the people accepting these children were only concerned with making a profit.

The 1920s and 1930s saw the beginnings of the most extensive reform in out-of-home care of children — the development of foster family homes as the major form of care and the breaking-down of large congregate institutions into smaller, more specialized group care units for children who were not well-suited for foster family living. These developments took place over several decades and reflected more knowledge about the welfare of children.

The elimination of old-style institutions serving large numbers of children was further accelerated in the 1950s, when a strong movement toward "deinstitutionalization" began. The first "community-based group homes" were opened in which workers undertook the care of small groups of children in ordinary dwelling houses in residential neighborhoods. Modern facilities, even large facilities, now work with children in small groups.

The period since the 1950s has been one of great growth. Programs reflecting a wide variety of psychological and social theories have been developed. More importantly, child care has made progress toward becoming a profession. Colleges and universities have developed child care programs. Agencies are beginning to hire more qualified people.

It is certainly much different for the children. There was admittedly a great deal of brutality in child care institutions in the past. Child care people from the old days will tell you that physical force was an everyday fact of life in institutions then. Although this problem has not been entirely solved, physical violence has been markedly reduced.

Things will be easier for you, too. You will probably find that your employer has a program designed to make your introduction to the field considerably easier.

TYPES OF GROUP CARE

Child care people do not have a single set of terms that they use to describe the various types of group care settings. Terminologies change from state to state and even from organization to organization. We can't untangle this for you; we'll simply try to give you definitions of some of the more commonly used terms.

Group Homes

Group homes are nearly always small communi-ty-based facilities located in family-type homes, usually in residential neighborhoods. Beyond this, a group home may be almost anything. The group home may serve emotionally disturbed children, offenders, handicapped children, children with fam-ily problems, or retarded children. The program offered might reflect any one of several treatment philosophies appropriate to the client population.

When child care people say "group home," they are usually referring to a certain type of "Mom and Pop" operation in which three or four staff mem-bers work with six to ten children.

Group home staff members often live in the home, at least part of the time. This type of care is, by the way, notoriously tough on staff members. Living with the children is *not* easy and requires considerable emotional and social stability.

Children's Centers

This term is not in use everywhere. Where it is, it refers to something larger than a group home but smaller than a big institution. It may have more than one "unit," "wing," "house," "floor," or "cottage," each with a distinct group of staff members and children, and would usually serve fewer than 50 children.

Centers whose entire program is directed toward treatment of a population of the more seriously emotionally disturbed children are often known as residential treatment centers.

Institutions

These are large operations, usually with one hundred or more beds. Children and staff members are divided into "units," "wings," "houses," "floors," or "cottages."

As a general rule, the larger a facility gets, the more specialized the staff becomes. Staff members in group homes are generally responsible for all aspects of the program. Staff members in children's centers have fewer, but still relatively general, responsibilities. In larger institutions, however, staff members may specialize in specific functions, such as recreation.

Big vs Small

A lot of people will tell you that all big institutions are bad for children. This isn't true, any more than it would be true to say that all small facilities are good for children.

The idea that "big is bad" originated when there were big congregate institutions that were really just warehouses. The children in these warehouses received little of the attention and affection people need in order to grow. Most are now closed. There are still, however, big facilities around, and some of them do a good job. To associate all big facilities with the old-style warehouses is unfair.

THE DIMENSION OF COMMUNITY

Group care settings are also described in terms of their integration into or isolation from the community. This, too, is confusing. After all, it's possible to see a farm as either isolated from the urban community or integrated into a rural community.

It is meaningful, however, to talk of facilities as either "open" or "closed." If it is open, it means that children can come and go much as they do in a normal family home. If it is closed, it means that children do not leave the grounds without adult supervision.

When a facility is described as "open and community-based," though, one runs into a problem. What is "community-based"? What is a "community," for that matter? In reality, group residences are located in nearly every conceivable neighborhood—in industrial parks, in rural areas, in suburban communities, in inner-city neighborhoods. The real question is whether the community is a good place for the children served. "Community-based" does imply that the agency uses local schools, recreational centers, parks, and other community resources. It also implies that it tries to maintain positive relationships with the surrounding community.

OTHER TYPES OF PROGRAMS

Although there are many different types of residential programs, here are two more general categories.

Secure Care

This form of care is used only for serious offenders and severely disturbed children. Secure programs are closed. Children may not leave the grounds. A number of different types of measures are taken to make sure that they don't. Locked doors and electronic security devices may be used. You should realize, however, that direct supervision by an adult is the only really reliable form of security. Dependence on anything else is dangerous.

Locked doors, in themselves, create dangers. Anything that might impede evacuation in an emergency is risky. Locked doors mean that all staff members *must* be alert and *must* know the emergency routines. Locked doors also create isolation. A secure unit is the whole world for the child locked inside. He or she has no alternative if the unit doesn't have adequate recreational resources; the child can't go and play in the park or visit friends or take a walk around the block. If the unit provides no opportunity for privacy, there is none. The only people the child sees are the other children and the staff.

If you work on a secure unit, try to imagine how it feels to be locked up or restricted in other ways from doing what you want to do. It will probably help you to be understanding of the pressures and tensions felt by the children.

Shelter Care

Shelter care is a temporary form of care. There are many different kinds of shelters. Runaway shelters provide children who run away from home with a "place to crash." Since a family crisis is frequently the reason why the child ran away, the runaway shelters usually work quickly with the family to help the child return home.

Diagnostic shelters keep children briefly in order to assess what they need. The child will be observed and given a variety of psychological and educational tests. Recommendations for the child's future will be based on the assessment. Child care staff members participate in the assessment process.

Shelters may be used to assist children and families in crisis, even though the child hasn't run away. A short shelter placement may help a child and family in conflict "cool off" and start working on their problems.

Shelters are also used to house minor offenders before they go to court.

Shelter care requires a lot from the child care staff member. There is constant turnover of children, since they don't stay long. It is unrealistic to expect lasting relationships with children in shelter care. There is usually not enough time to build the kind of relationships that bring about lasting internal change. However, the child care worker must give all he or she can in the way of caring and nurturance—and the giving must happen immediately. It is hard to make an instantaneous investment in a child you don't know, but such is the nature of shelter care.

WHAT KIND OF CHILD LIVES IN A RESIDENTIAL SETTING?

Residential settings also serve different types of children, but all have serious problems, otherwise they wouldn't be in group care. Whenever possible, children who can adjust to a family are placed with a foster family. The children in residential care are those for whom foster family care is either impossible or inappropriate.

You often hear people say things like, "You can't blame the kids. It's really the parents who are at fault." The fact is that special children come from all types of families. Most of these families have tried hard to care for their children. It isn't fair and it doesn't help to blame parents. It is true that some of the parents of children with emotional problems have emotional problems themselves. It's true that some of the children have been neglected or abused. It's also true that finding someone to blame is not a particularly constructive way of solving problems.

Let's look at some of the "special children" in group care.

Delinquents

In recent years the term "juvenile delinquent" has fallen into disuse. In most states it has been replaced by "offenders" or "young offenders." Offenders are people who have broken the law. The courts do not place offenders in closed residential facilities unless the offenses are serious and/or repeated.

In the old days children were sent to correctional institutions or "schools" for first offenses, and sometimes for very minor offenses. It was enough, in some states, to be picked up riding in a stolen car or to be truant from school. This is no longer the case. The courts have come to the realization that locking children up, unless it is absolutely necessary, creates more problems than it solves. Once a child has been placed in a closed correctional facility, the chances of the child having continuing problems with the law are greatly increased.

Modern correctional settings, whether closed or open, don't look or act like jails. Staff members are not expected to adopt a prison guard mentality. Things aren't done by the numbers. Correctional settings often look just like any other residential facilities.

Status offenders and children who have committed minor offenses are generally not mixed with persons who have committed more serious offenses. There is a sound reason for this. In the past the mixing of such populations caused minor and status offenders to join a criminal subculture and increased the chances of future serious offenses.

The "offenders" label is a serious one. What it amounts to, like it or not, is calling a child a criminal. If you call a child a criminal, the child will try to oblige by being a criminal. The courts have become increasingly careful about labeling children, as they should be.

Emotionally Disturbed Children

These are children with mental health problems. Since a discussion of these problems is beyond the scope of this book, we'll leave it at that. Anyone who works in a mental health or residential treatment center will learn from other sources about the different types of emotional disturbance and the labels applied to them. We should note, however, that many of these children are "children who hate." They may show a lot of hostility toward workers. Needless to say, those who work with this population should be very emotionally stable.

Despite the fact that mental health or residential treatment centers use social workers, psychologists, and psychiatrists, child care workers have a key role in treatment programs. As a matter of fact, in some agencies the child care worker is perceived as the primary therapist. Many children in all forms of residential treatment see the child care worker as a person they talk to if they have a problem.

Dependent/Neglected/Abused

Dependent/neglected/abused children are children with family problems. In many cases these children are placed in foster family care. If the child has special problems or if it seems likely that the family may be reunited in the future, the child may be placed in group care.

Actually, children with family problems frequently have emotional problems. A child care worker may have to deal with the same types of problems as a worker in a mental health center. Generally speaking, though, these problems will be less severe.

Retarded and Autistic Children

These children require specialized care that is different in many respects from the type of care

described in this book. Specialized facilities will
provide the appropriate training.

Labels

All these categories are labels. You will discover
many more labels after you have worked in the
field for a while. Just remember: There are people
under those labels and each person is unique.
Don't substitute the label for the child.

2

Your First Day on the Job

Old child care workers like to tell horror stories about what it was like to be a beginning child care worker in the old days. At one time they just gave you a ring of keys, showed you how to sign in, and turned you loose with immediate responsibility for twenty or thirty children. Fortunately, things have changed considerably. Most facilities go to great trouble to orient new workers and know that it will take months of training before you are able to be a fully functioning member of the child care team. They are prepared to invest time and resources to help you become a professional.

No one really expects you to be very useful on your first day. They will probably appreciate you most if you concentrate on listening and don't get underfoot. For some strange reason, a lot of new workers try to give the impression that they know it all. This is probably just a normal reaction to an insecure situation, but nothing is more likely to turn off more experienced staff members.

17

Just remember: your job, for the moment, is to learn how to do your job.

How are you feeling?

You're probably a little scared. That's perfectly natural. The best way to handle your fear is to be properly prepared and to know a little about what you are in for.

WHAT HAPPENS ON THE FIRST DAY?

We can't really tell you that. You should ask the person who hired you if he or she has not fully informed you.

Usually you will meet the children and some of the other staff members. Usually you will get a tour of the facility and a rundown of your responsibilities. In particular, you will probably get a rundown of safety practices. The facility will usually assign an experienced worker to show you the ropes. It is likely to be some time before you are on your own with the children.

Relating to Other Staff Members

As noted previously, other staff members are likely to resent you if you give them the message that you know it all.

Child care workers tend, for a number of reasons, to form very tight groups that may be hard to penetrate. Shared interests and schedules mean that child care people tend to spend time-off together. Besides that, working with other people in child care is a far more intimate situation than it would be in most other jobs. Residential child care is an activity that creates a family atmosphere. A group of workers who have been together for a while will be almost as close as a family. And you are a new member of this family. You cannot expect immediate acceptance.

It's always good to know whom you are replacing. You may be taking the place of someone who was very much a part of the family. To be honest, this will make things more difficult for you. The other staff members and, of course, the kids, may resent your replacing "good old Joe." However unfair this may be, it's a natural reaction and is best left alone to run its course. You may get tired of hearing how good "good old Joe" was compared to you. It will stop eventually.

Other staff members may want to be sure that you intend to stay. They may adopt a "wait-and-see" attitude toward you. You may have to be patient until they are ready to accept you.

On the whole, you will find that child care people are very good people. Because of the nature of their work, they are inclined to talk problems out and deal honestly with others. You will probably make some lasting friends.

Meeting the Children

The children may be slow to accept you, for the same reasons as the staff members. They will probably be much less gentle about it. They may say, "I don't like you. You're not like Joe," or "You won't last a week here." All they are really saying is that they miss Joe and are afraid that you will leave just as he did. Here, again, patience is the best policy.

Some children may approach you and treat you like a long-lost friend. Do not fall into the trap of assuming that you have formed a "meaningful relationship" on your first day. Children who have difficulty forming relationships often learn to exploit relative strangers and superficial relationships to get some of the good feelings denied to them in long-term relationships. This does not mean that you should reject such approaches. It would be well, though, not to assume that you have made a great breakthrough.

Some children may try to con you. You don't know the rules nor do you have any idea of their past behavior. They may ask you if they can do something that they know very well the other staff members would not allow. If a child asks you a question and you really don't know the answer, don't feel that you will "lose face" if you ask someone. As a matter of fact, you are going to be in a lot of trouble with everyone if you fail to ask questions. The children will take advantage of this weakness and the other staff members will be angry with you for the resulting confusion.

Experienced child care workers try to avoid assuming a lot of control over the children for the first few days of a new job. They try to observe the situation and learn something about the children and other staff members before they attempt any exercise of authority. Inexperienced workers are more likely to try to establish themselves too quickly.

On your first day you will be meeting a large number of new people. It will probably take several days just to keep their names straight. Don't expect to make a big impression. Just be patient, calm, and concentrate on getting to know them. The children, and everyone else, will respect you for that.

What Should You Know?

There are several questions that you should be able to answer about your job. Make sure that you get the answers to these questions as soon as possible if you don't have them already.

1. Who is your boss? How do you fit into the organizational chart?
2. What is your job? What are you supposed to do and not to do?
3. What should you do in case of a fire, accident, or other emergency?
4. What type of child is served by this agency and what services does the agency provide?

There is, of course, a great deal more to know, but having clear answers to these questions is absolutely essential.

What Should You Wear?

Child care administrators often complain about the way child care workers dress, particularly new workers. One administrator remarked, "They either show up dressed for a shift in the coal mines or they dress for a cocktail party."

Depending on the children served, the child care worker's job can be messy. Fancy dress is definitely out. Sexy or provocative dress is definitely out. On the other hand, you do want to set a good example. Something moderate, practical, and relatively rugged is called for.

A comfortable pair of shoes is a good idea. You will often spend a whole shift on your feet.

Keys

You may be given a set of keys to locked storage spaces and, in some instances, to doors within the facility. These keys are your responsibility and should not be lent to anyone — particularly not to children.

Storage spaces often contain harmful substances. They are locked up as a safety precaution. Don't get careless with the keys. Experienced child care workers generally find a way to have the keys on their persons at all times, for example, fastened to a chain around the neck or to a belt loop.

Smoking

If you are a smoker, you had best find out your agency's policies on smoking before you start work. Child care institutions tend to have a large number of rules governing smoking. Some agencies allow children to smoke and some don't. Those that don't usually have a big problem with violations of this rule. Most agencies just have areas where smoking is not allowed. You must observe the rule about these areas.

It is not a good idea to give cigarettes to children. The moral issue aside, you probably cannot afford it. If you start supplying cigarettes, there will be no end to it. In any case, many agencies frown on this practice.

If the kids are not allowed to smoke and you are, you may expect several thousand hours of argument about the unfairness of this policy.

Modes of Address

In some agencies, it is conventional to call other staff members "Mrs. so-and-so" or "Mr. so-and-so." Often, the children are required to use these modes of address, although they are probably addressed by their first names. Most agencies are considerably less formal; everyone is called by their first names.

THE NIGHT AFTER THE FIRST DAY

How was it?

If it was frightening and confusing, don't worry. Most new child care workers report that kind of experience on their first day. It gets easier. If it was good, you got lucky. You also may just be on the honeymoon. It may get harder.

It may be the beginning of a beautiful experience.

3
Guarding Life

As a child care worker your *first* responsibility is to protect the safety of the children.

Unfortunately, many workers and some agencies do not place much emphasis on this aspect of the job. The lack of safety consciousness can have the most serious consequences imaginable. It can result in death or serious injury. Be safety conscious!

Most agencies do have safety rules, evacuation plans, and even disaster plans. Fire, medical, and other safety professionals warn us that appropriate safety and emergency procedures depend on the environment of the facility. Something that makes good sense in one facility might be totally wrong in another. You have to study yours.

The kind of child served by your agency is a cardinal consideration. Each child has a different capacity to protect his or her own life. A severely disturbed child or a retarded child would obviously be potentially more endangered than other children.

The type of program offered by the residence is also an important consideration. Locked doors, for example, impede evacuation in the event of an emergency. If persons in other settings should be safety conscious, the staff in a locked facility should be *obsessed* with safety.

Safety isn't just a matter of potential emergencies like fires or earthquakes. Child care workers are responsible for the general health of children. Like a parent, you have to be alert for signs of illness or injury. It is especially desirable that you be qualified to do basic first aid.

"EYEBALLING"

The essence of safety consciousness is alertness. At the beginning of your workday you should have a close look at the children and the environment. Take a slow walking tour through the facility, checking that everyone is healthy and everything is as it should be.

Check the exits to make sure that each is clear and operational.

Check the fire equipment. Extinguishers have a little gauge on them that shows if they are fully charged. Since kids get a real kick out of discharging them, check these gauges daily. You would look awfully silly pointing an empty extinguisher at a fire. It *has* happened.

Note and correct any unsafe conditions—exposed wiring, loose flooring, and so on.

If you make a habit of "eyeballing" the environment and the kids, after a while you will do it without thinking about it. It's a good habit. Speaking of habits, many child care workers develop the habit of saying "How are you feeling?" to everyone they meet. That's because the best way to check on the children's condition is to ask them.

FIRE

You probably already know a great deal about fire prevention. The common-sense rules that apply in any household apply in your facility. The trick, as always, is to keep sources of heat away from things that burn, and vice versa.

Fortunately, most residences are well equipped. They have smoke detectors and heat detectors and automatic alarm systems with emergency power sources. They have fire escapes and fire exits. They are constructed with the least flammable materials in the safest possible way. Many have fire doors.

A word about fire doors. A surprising number of people don't know what they are. A fire door is a solidly constructed door designed to stop a fire from spreading. They only work, of course, if they're closed. In some facilities people who don't want to be bothered opening doors all the time use gate hooks or door stops to keep them open. A fire door is designed to be closed — that's why it's equipped with an automatic closer. Don't circumvent this safety device.

You may be wondering what all this elaborate equipment is for. Anywhere you have children, you also have fire danger. Children *like* fire. They are also more likely to panic and get seriously injured if a fire occurs.

Fire Prevention

Because of its design, there are usually few fire risks in a facility. Let's identify the areas you should "eyeball."

Storage Areas   As you would in your own home, make sure that your storage areas don't contain piles of newspapers, oily rags, or other flammables. Keep them neat and make sure that solvents or other flammable liquids are stored in tight cans away from any heat source. Do not use the furnace room for storage. Doors on storage areas should be locked at all times.

Wiring   Frayed or damaged wiring should be reported and replaced. Extension cords in use should be checked for signs of wear.

Children's Rooms   Most facilities don't allow smoking in children's sleeping areas. They also don't allow candles, electric heaters, or other such heat sources. These are sensible precautions. See that they're carried out.

The Kitchen   In facilities, as in homes, the kitchen is a major source of fires. If you cook, keep the oven clean and be careful with oil and grease. The kitchen should have an extinguisher rated for grease and oil fires. And, of course, don't store flammables near the stove.

The Fire Alarm System   Make sure you find out how your system works. On your first day at work, ask someone to show you. Pay close attention to their instructions on how to turn it off in the event of a false alarm. Any automatic system makes mistakes. If the system has pull boxes, there's also the possibility of intentional false alarms. If there are no pull boxes, there are still ways to set off an alarm—and the kids usually know them. A rag soaked in hot water from the tap applied directly to a heat detector will do the trick every time. Similarly, a piece of burning paper directly underneath a smoke detector will trip the alarm. You are going to be in an embarrassing position if, after determining that it's a false alarm, you don't know how to turn off the bells. You will be hearing *that* story for years.

By the way, if your facility has a system with an emergency power source (usually a series of batteries that automatically kick in when the current's off), periodically "eyeball" the power pack to make sure that it is safely charged. The power system will have a conveniently labeled gauge for you to check.

Fire alarm systems *must* be periodically checked to make sure that everything is working. This need not be done daily, but should happen at least weekly. You do this by hitting a "trouble" or "test" switch and listening for the bells. This is usually done by a staff safety officer.

Drills   Unfortunately, no one has ever invented an alternative to the fire drill. The best way to ensure that an evacuation can be carried out safely is to practice it.

Kids and staff alike sometimes feel that fire drills are "Mickey Mouse" stuff. There's nothing like a real fire to make a believer out of you. Take the drills seriously and try to see that the kids do. As a staff member, it's important for you to know what your assignment is during an evacuation. Drills remind you.

Evacuation   Most residences have evacuation plans. Staff members are assigned to ensure evacuation of particular areas and, of course, someone calls the fire department. Make sure that you know what you are supposed to do.

The details of evacuation depend on the type of structure. In multistoried dwellings, evacuation of the upper stories is usually by fire escapes. Elevators, if they exist, are *not* used for fire evacuations.

The basic rule is to get the kids outside by the most direct, safe route. In the upper stories of a small building, this is usually the fire escape. Even if the central staircase is not involved in the fire, do not use it unless exit by the fire escape is blocked.

To live through a fire, you have to get to the open air. Persons who die in fires are rarely burned to death. Smoke inhalation is the major cause of fatality.

In an orderly evacuation all doors and windows should be closed. Lack of air supply slows down a fire's spread.

It is your responsibility to check your area to make sure that everyone is out. Then it's a good idea to get yourself out. Child care workers aren't fireproof.

Once outside, a head count should be made immediately. You have to determine that everyone has been evacuated. If someone is missing, do not reenter the building but report it to the fire department. Likewise, prevent your children from re-entering the building no matter *what* they've left behind.

Real Fires

If a small fire occurs in a single locality, you should consider the possibility of putting it out. Fire officials tell us that many buildings are severely damaged by fires that some clear-thinking individual *could* have put out with an extinguisher. (But entering a room of raging fire with a fire extinguisher is complete foolishness. Smoke is dangerous.) You also have to know what type of extinguisher you're using. Putting water on an electrical or grease fire will have spectacular, but not particularly desirable, results.

Evacuation of the children is *always* the first priority. Notification of the fire department comes a very close second.

In a real fire it is a bad idea to run around throwing doors open to see that everyone is out. You may open the door to a room with a fire in it. If you suspect this, place your palm on the door to feel for heat.

Second to smoke, panic is probably the major killer. In most cases, everyone in a building has time to be evacuated without too much hurry. Moving down most fire escapes in a rush is dangerous.

OTHER DISASTERS

A residence must have plans for dealing with the kinds of disasters likely to occur in the locality. This varies from one area to another across the country.

Many facilities, like many American households, are well prepared for emergencies. Many have stocks of food, water, medical supplies, and other necessities. Some have equipped emergency shelters, emergency light systems, and a variety of other supplies.

It is up to you to be thoroughly familiar with the plans and resources of your agency.

BUILDING SAFETY

The really major danger in a facility is the same as it is in any household. Accidents around the home account for many serious injuries. The list of dangers is almost endless. To prevent the common household accident, you have to have a sharp eye out for hazards. Some hazards look perfectly harmless—common but highly toxic household substances carelessly stored; faulty wiring; sharp projections of corners; loose rugs, particularly on staircases; slippery surfaces; faulty equipment.

You probably have a number of unsafe conditions in your own home. You know what they are and how to avoid them. The more people you have in an environment, however, the more dangerous such minor defects become.

When you spot an unsafe condition, correct it immediately, if possible, or report it to the person responsible for maintenance. Replacement or repair of broken or defective equipment or furnishings is important. Aside from safety considerations, there is no surer way to encourage vandalism than to allow the environment to deteriorate.

HEALTH

You are responsible for the children's health.

This responsibility is similar to the responsibility you might feel as a parent. You are responsible for the child's general health—hygiene, diet, and so on, and for noticing if the child is sick or injured. Here again, the "eyeballing" method is very useful. Be alert for sluggishness, irritability, and other signs of physical or mood changes.

Diet

There is absolutely no doubt that diet affects a child's behavior. There is considerable argument about what the best diet is, but there is very little disagreement that certain eating habits are harmful.

You will find that many children in your care eat poorly. Some, it would seem, prefer a diet of soda, candy bars, french fries, and other junk food. If you don't recognize what kind of effect this would have on your system, try it for a few days.

Many children are virtually addicted to sugar. Taking large quantities of sugar can produce effects quite similar to those produced by some drugs—periods of high energy followed by depression. Some teachers claim that the day after Halloween, when children generally overdose on candy, is the worst day of the year. Our experience would bear this out.

Few children will eat anything like a balanced diet. Many absolutely refuse vegetables in any form. Some overeat. Troubled children generally have a lot of problems in this area.

The giving of food is certainly one of the most fundamental expressions of caring. Likewise, withholding of a balanced meal from a child is the ultimate rejection.

Preaching at people about what they eat is not very effective. The best way is to set a good example.

Hygiene

Children will not automatically remember to take baths, change their clothes, and brush their teeth. As a matter of fact, many preadolescent children go through a stage when they are down-right hostile to good hygiene and grooming. Seeing that they do these things is one of the more troublesome parts of your job.

For a little while it may be difficult for you to remember these things. You may also find it embarrassing to tell someone, even a child, to take a bath or change his or her socks. The direct approach is best. Teaching children proper groom-ing and hygiene is part of your job. Remember, though, not to impose your personal taste in hair style or similar things.

For many children, learning to be clean and well groomed helps change the way they feel about themselves and, incidentally, how others feel about them.

Vermin

Like public schools, facilities have occasional problems with lice, fleas, and bedbugs. We hate to have to tell you this but we should stress that, although it's a rare problem, it does occur.

Fleas leave little bites very much like mosquito bites. They can be eliminated with a good bath and some special shampoo. (It's a little embarrassing asking for it at the drug store but it works!)

Lice can be detected by the inflammation and itching they cause on the scalp. Take suspected cases to a nurse.

Bedbugs leave telltale tiny spots of blood on bedding. They spread like wildfire. Eggs can be transmitted from place to place in clothing. Nothing short of a massive fumigation and cleaning and airing of bedding and mattresses will stop them. Your local health department can give further suggestions.

Other Health Problems

You have to monitor the health of the children in your care. If you are at all uncertain about a child's health, get him or her to the doctor. Make a written note of any health problem you encounter to make sure that other staff members know of it.

You should be aware that there is presently a virtual epidemic of various forms of venereal disease (V.D.). Most cases of V.D. may be quickly and easily treated. The problem is that young people are often unwilling to report the symptoms. Considering the considerable effort that has been made to educate the public, most people are remarkably ignorant about V.D. It is still a topic that most people are reluctant to discuss. If any of the residents complain of pain or discomfort in the genital region, get them to a doctor.

MEDICAL EMERGENCIES

You have to be ready to think and act quickly if someone is seriously ill or injured. Most residences post a list of emergency numbers by the telephone. You should keep a copy of this list with you at all times.

Many people in the field believe that every child care worker should take a first aid course. Courses are available from a variety of sources; many are free. We recommend that you take the time to do this.

Poisoning Poisoning is a fairly common medical emergency. Make sure that your list of emergency numbers includes the Poison Control number. This agency can tell you what to do for a specific type of poisoning until the ambulance gets there. Many types of poisoning require *immediate* treatment. Treatment indicated for one type of poisoning may be harmful for the victim of another type of poisoning.

Suicide Some children are serious risks to themselves. You should know if any of your children have made a previous attempt at suicide. Children generally make numerous efforts to communicate what they are about to do before attempting suicide. Threats of suicide should always be listened to. Try to prevent the occurrence. Know the emergency procedures.

CAR SAFETY

Workers are frequently required to drive children around. Sometimes you may find yourself with a number of children in your vehicle. This is a heavy responsibility. If you are at all unsure of your driving, take a professional driving course.

Children seem to have a tendency to become playful and to get into arguments and even fights in cars, vans, and buses. This is not only irritating, it is dangerous. The driver should pay attention to driving, not to refereeing. Set up the ground rules before you start the car. We always make the following speech: "I can't drive safely with people making noise. I don't mind if you talk quietly but if you get loud or start to argue with each other, I'm going to pull the car over until you quiet down. Does everyone understand what I mean?"

In any vehicle carrying a large number of children, it is best to have at least two staff members. Insist on seat belts!

SWIMMING

Never, under any circumstances, take children swimming without a certified lifeguard or in an area posted as unsafe for swimming. Insist that your children follow *all* safety rules given by the lifeguard.

4
Finding Your Way

If guarding the health and safety of children is the primary responsibility of all child care workers, what are their other responsibilities?

Child care work is, above all else, a job. Your facility pays you a salary to perform certain specified duties and to be present and ready for work during specified hours. Like other workers, you are required to do some paperwork, write some reports, and account for any money you spend on the facility's behalf.

Child care workers tend to forget this. They tend to regard child care work as a "mission," as more than a job. The informality of the work situation as well contributes to a lax attitude toward certain job responsibilities.

Nearly every child care worker in existence hates paperwork. There is something about working directly with people all day that makes it hard to fill out forms and write reports. But paperwork is important because the agency must keep track of what you're doing. This is the only way it can run a reasonably businesslike operation and plan for the future. As well, other workers need to know what you are doing with a particular child.

Your responsibilities will depend on the agency and every agency has its own way of doing things. This chapter will not provide you with all the answers to the question of what the agency expects of you. It will only help you to ask the right questions to find these answers.

WORKING HOURS

Residences schedule working hours in a variety of ways. Whatever your residence does, it is essential that you be on time for work. In most jobs being late for work displeases the boss but doesn't have serious consequences unless you make a habit of it. In child care work, one or more of your co-workers will have to stay on until you arrive. After working a long hard shift, all you need is for your relief to be a half-hour late. Being late to relieve fellow workers is one of the surest ways to become unpopular. Other workers will resent your lateness and probably tell you so. They may also start arriving late for *your* relief.

If you have to be late for some reason, call in and let people know. It's a good policy to offer to come in early for the next shift. Other workers will note that you take your responsibilities seriously.

Live-In

Some facilities employ live-in staff members, often a married couple, with one or more workers who may or may not live in. Usually, relief workers are employed to give live-in staff time off. Some facilities use a modified arrangement in which workers live in for part of the week.

Living at the facility is not easy. It means intense, around-the-clock involvement. If you stay in during time off you are *very* likely to be disturbed constantly by the children and the relief staff. It's a good idea to get away as much as possible.

For couples, live-in work is a notorious source of marital problems. They spend a great deal of time together and have very little time alone. Marital breakdowns are a relatively frequent occurrence. This type of work is only for very stable and secure couples who have been together for some time.

Singles living at facilities also have problems. It is difficult to maintain any kind of social life. Your schedule just won't match the schedules of friends in conventional jobs. Again, emotional stability is required.

Shift Work

This is now the most common type of child care.

Many facilities use what is known as a "swing shift." The day is broken into three eight-hour shifts—7 A.M. to 3 P.M.; 3 P.M. to 11 P.M.; 11 P.M. to 7 A.M. These are informally known as day shift, evening shift, and night or "graveyard" shift.

Workers may work days one week and evenings the next. In some cases, they may work the night shift the following week. Some facilities have a worker or workers who always work the night shift; in this instance, other workers alternate between days and evenings. In some places workers may have "straight days" or "straight evenings." This means that they always work the same shift.

A swing shift, where you change your working hours every week, takes a lot of getting used to. For several weeks you will have trouble sleeping, particularly when you are on night shift. It just doesn't seem right to be going to bed when every one else is going to work.

Working the night shift is both tiring and boring. Your major responsibility is staying awake in case something happens, and possibly making periodic rounds. It may involve just sitting at a desk all night. If you are on night shift and are not required to do anything else, bring along something to do. If you try to just sit there, you are bound to fall asleep. Books and handicrafts will help.

Some workers claim that a sleeping mask helps solve the problem of sleeping in daylight.

Shift Change

Most residences schedule a brief meeting when one group of workers takes over from another. This is even true if staff members live in the facility.

It is good to have a regular routine for starting work. An experienced worker usually arrives a little early to have extra time to get oriented.

As you come into the building, make it a practice *never* to deal with any problem or question posed by the children until *after* shift change. You have to know the situation before you make any decisions.

After signing in, you should have enough time to read the log before the shift-change meeting. The log is a written diary of events during the previous shift. Make notes of any situations requiring action during your shift, particularly any restrictions applied to individual children—for example, if two kids had a fight before going to school, you will have to deal with it when they return. Or, if the kitchen sink is clogged, it may be up to you to call a repairman.

Nobody wants a shift change meeting to drag on forever. If you are being relieved, tell the new shift only what they need to know. They don't want to hear a long, rambling account of your day. They want to know what shape the kids are in, what problems you have had, and what actions they should take during their shift. Other workers will love you for conducting a brief, effective shift change.

Following shift change, an experienced worker makes an "eyeballing" tour of the facility.

MEETINGS

Attendance at meetings is an important responsibility of your job. Meetings are held for:

- training and supervision
- handling administrative matters
- sharing information
- planning for individual children and the group

Frequently, the facility holds only one meeting each week. This meeting is used for all of the

above purposes and attendance is absolutely essential. It's also important, once again, to be on
time. Everyone hates waiting for latecomers.

It's a good idea to keep your comments brief
and to the point. Many child care workers have
the annoying habit of telling long and pointless stories at meetings. Always make sure that there is
some *reason* for your comments.

Supervision Meetings

Some agencies make a practice of holding periodic meetings between the supervisor and each
worker. These meetings are designed to help the
worker identify his or her strengths and weaknesses. Supervisory meetings also provide an opportunity to blow off steam about the job.

Your supervisor cannot help you unless you are
reasonably honest about how you feel. A good
supervisor will realize how uncomfortable it is to
discuss your performance with him or her and will
try to help you feel that you can look forward to
these meetings as a chance to discuss the job with
someone who knows the pressures first-hand and
can help you.

Evaluation Meetings

Once or twice a year, most agencies hold an
evaluation conference with each worker. At this
conference, supervisory personnel discuss your
job performance with you. It's a little bit like getting a report card. It's unlikely, though, that your
supervisor will tell you anything that you haven't
heard already.

An evaluation conference can be particularly useful to you. It can help you identify the things that you're good at and the things that you need to work on. Many supervisors afford the worker the opportunity to participate in the evaluation process. If you are encouraged to offer your opinion, take full advantage of the opportunity without getting into a struggle of wills with your supervisor.

SPECIAL TRAINING ACTIVITIES

Many agencies schedule special training activities, which may involve sending staff members to a series of lectures or workshops or to a child care conference.

Some agencies are very open to helping workers improve job-related skills. They encourage and provide incentives for workers interested in continuing education, in first-aid courses, or in other learning activities. We know of one facility that will provide workers with time off to get bus-driving licenses. (By the way, workers with bus-driving licenses, swimming certificates, and first-aid certificates are *always* in demand.) Some agencies require that all child care workers have a current driver's license. If you're smart, you will take as much advantage of such opportunities as possible.

PAPERWORK

As noted earlier, child care workers, like employees in virtually every type of business and industry, are required to do paperwork. We devote a separate chapter to it (chapter 8), but let us take note here that child care paperwork generally has one or more of the following purposes:

- recording of information required for the administration of the facility
- reporting and analyzing the behavior of a child or group of children
- sharing information with other workers

Keeping your paperwork up-to-date is a demonstration that you are a responsible employee.

THE LOG

Virtually every facility in existence keeps a running daily log, which can range from simple affairs to complex systems. The simplest kind of log is the plain old "rummage log." This is basically just a diary. Each shift writes in what has happened under the day's date.

Some facilities also keep individual logs for each child. In most cases, the individual log has a daily check list and space for comments. This may include the daily computation of "points" for good behavior, where such systems are in use.

Some facilities also use an "administrative log." This contains any action that must be taken by the next shift. It might include instructions on items to be purchased, household repairs needed, phone calls to be made, and similar entries.

Although chapter 8 includes log and report writing, let us say, for now, that written communications should be brief and to the point. Log entries should, however, describe what happened during the entire shift.

REPORTS

Child care workers are sometimes asked to complete reports on particular children or other matters. If, for instance, a child is injured or is "in crisis," you may be asked to describe the events leading up to the situation.

PETTY CASH AND OTHER ACCOUNTING

Most facilities have a petty cash system for small purchases. You must account for each purchase, which usually involves filling out a petty cash receipt and subtracting the amount spent from a running total.

Whether or not your employer requires it, it is a good practice to "cash up" at the beginning and end of each shift. You simply count the money, make sure that it is correct, and enter a notation to that effect in the petty cash book, along with the time and your signature. The truth is that the petty cash systems in many facilities are in perpetual turmoil. People are always forgetting to make the correct entries. By "cashing up" at the beginning and end of your shift, you can save yourself a lot of trouble when someone starts trying to trace the source of a shortage.

Agencies use a myriad of accounting practices for larger purchases. If you are required to pur-

chase food, clothing, or other supplies on behalf of
the facility, make sure that you understand what
you must do.

Mileage

Many agencies pay mileage if you use your car
on agency business. Basically, you get reimbursed
so many cents for each mile traveled. At the end of
each week you turn in a mileage form showing the
number of miles traveled and what the facility
owes you.

If you are paid mileage, make a wise investment.
Buy a clipboard. Tape a piece of string to the clipboard and tie a pen to the string. Put your agency's mileage form on the clipboard, along with several sheets of paper ruled into two columns. Use
the ruled paper to note the figures on your car's
odometer at the beginning and end of each trip.
Subtract the first figure from the second to get the
total number of miles traveled. Fill in the mileage
form as you go along. At the end of the week, all
you have to do is total it up and sign it. If you don't
do this, you will end up losing track awfully fast.

While we're on the subject, it's also a good idea
to invest in a zipper wallet and a notebook that will
fit inside it. Keep this with your clipboard and use
it to record any purchases you make for the facility. Slip the receipts into the wallet. This will keep
your receipts from getting lost. Now you're organized!

Make sure, also, that you understand your
agency's practices regarding auto insurance cov-
erage (as well as other kinds of liability insurances).

WHO'S ON FIRST?

It's very important that you know what the various persons who work at your agency do. Since you are part of a team it's essential that you work well with others. Agencies arrange their staffs in many different ways. Below are some of the more common jobs.

Chief Executive or Executive Director

This, of course, is the boss. Much of his or her time is probably spent making sure that your paycheck doesn't bounce. Executive directors of private operations, in particular, spend a lot of time setting up the budget, dealing with funding sources, and raising money. The executive director also works with the board of directors, if there is one, and, with them, plans the future of the agency. The executive director also spends a great deal of time handling problems brought to him or her by the staff and overseeing the smooth running of all departments.

Assistant Director

In most facilities the assistant director is like the executive officer on a ship. He or she is directly involved in translating the boss's directives into action. The assistant director is usually involved in supervising the program, more or less directly, and working directly with the staff.

Director of Residential Life

This job appears only in fairly large facilities and consists of the overall direction of the entire child

care staff. The director of residential life will probably become involved in any serious problems in
the residences or cottages.

Child Care Supervisor

This person is the on-site supervisor. He or she
usually works at the residence and directly super-
vises child care workers. This is the person to call
on when you have a problem.

Recreation Worker

This person, sometimes an unpaid volunteer,
provides recreational programs for the children.

Tutor

Tutors are also often unpaid volunteers. They
help individual children with schoolwork.

Psychologist

Psychologists may or may not be members of
the staff. In some cases they are freelance professionals who sell their services to the facility. Some
psychologists specialize entirely in giving psychological and intelligence tests. Others conduct therapy with children, with groups of children, or with
families.

Psychiatrist

Psychiatrists also may be on the staff of some
facilities. Psychiatrists assess children and work
with individuals and groups in therapy. Psychia-

trists are also medical doctors and can prescribe drugs.

Social Worker

A social worker collects "social histories"—descriptions of a child's past and family background. Social workers work with families as well as with children, referral sources, licensing authorities, schools, and so forth. Social workers are a good resource to you and you are their resource in knowing about the day-to-day functioning of a child.

Support Staff

This is the well-chosen term for clerical and maintenance staff members. Without them, how long could the residence run or the professionals do their jobs? They have a double importance in child care centers, however. As on-grounds personnel, they are in constant contact with the children and they and the children have a special meaning for each other. In some centers, the treatment team plans ways in which specific support staff members can be helpful to particular children.

Volunteers

We have already briefly mentioned volunteers. In one sense, the board of directors consists of volunteers. But residences have a long history of seeking volunteers for activities from direct help for children to fund raising to clerical assistance, according to the volunteers' individual interests and skills. They enrich the program at all times, but in hard times, especially, they may be essential.

Paid workers have in the past sometimes been tense and resentful in the presence of volunteers out of fear for their own job security. Long experience has taught that this is an idle fear. Employees have learned that volunteers are a welcome help to themselves and the children.

Medical Help

All child welfare agencies must have medical help—doctor, nurse, hospital—readily available. The arrangements are myriad, in light of the great variety of agencies, their localities, and so on. Medical personnel may be on staff or on call or stationed in the community. It would be a good thing for you to get a quick grasp of the setup in your organization.

Agencies also usually have some kind of provision for dental work.

EXTRA DUTIES

Most agencies assign extra duties to each child care worker, based on his or her interests and abilities.

One worker in a residence is usually designated the safety officer, who is responsible for conducting fire drills, checking safety equipment, and generally overseeing the safety program.

One worker usually handles the money and is responsible for the petty cash, clothing money, food money, and so on. This is a harrowing and thankless task, but someone has to do it.

In facilities where child care staff members are involved in cooking, one person may be responsible for food purchasing and planning meals. This responsibility may also be shared.

Some facilities may assign child care staff members as prime workers for particular children. For the children who are your responsibility, you see that they are being properly cared for and appropriately treated.

Some facilities also assign a particular worker to act as "school liaison." This means that you stay in contact with community schools attended by the children and ensure close cooperation between school and facility. Some residences have an on-grounds school. Social workers may also carry the school-liaison function.

FINDING YOUR WAY

A residential facility is like any other organization. Each one has a slightly different way of doing things. The important thing is to find out what policies your facility has—what *your* job entails.

No facility has ever devised the perfect orientation for new workers. There are so many details involved in the running of a facility that even if it were possible to tell you everything you need to know, you couldn't possibly remember all of it.

In the end, you have to learn as you work. Nobody gets everything right the first time. The important thing is that you know what questions to ask.

5

The Routine

Your next most important duty, after guarding the safety of the children and finding your way around, is the most basic child care skill—supervision of children. Much of your working day will be spent in this activity. For the professional child care worker, talking about problems with children and about the exciting and dramatic types of encounters many people associate with our type of work takes a back seat to something universally called the "routine."

The routine contains all the ordinary business of a child's life—getting up, going to school, coming home, having dinner, relaxing, and going to bed. A good routine is an orderly and hassle-free way of life.

Unfortunately, routine has come to be almost a bad word in our society. We associate routine with mindless, dull, and regimented activities. Inexperienced workers tend to regard the routine as the least important part of their job. They couldn't be more wrong.

The routine at a residence is generally designed to teach children the habits necessary for survival in our society. The routine provides a safe, predictable environment for people to work on their problems. Perhaps most important, the routine ensures that everyone is rested, properly nourished, and well cared for. *Nothing* is more important than the routine.

Stop for a moment and consider how much of your life is spent in routine activities and how important routine is to you. If it weren't for the routine of getting up, showering, shaving or putting on makeup, and going to work, you couldn't hold down a job. You don't stop to think about any of these things, you just do them. Preparing food, washing dishes, paying bills, and all forms of housework are routines. A person—any person—who doesn't have good routines is in serious trouble.

So much of our social behavior is routine that one might be led to believe that nothing else exists. When you meet a co-worker you say, "Hi, how are you?" He or she says, "Fine. You?" The cashier gives you your change and you say, "Thank you." You're at a party and you turn to the person next to you and say, "What do you do?"

The routine at the facility teaches children all these things—how to behave appropriately in our society. You may privately think that "appropriate behavior" isn't the important thing. Try surviving without it. Your ability to put yourself on automatic pilot and behave like a good citizen, a responsible employee, and a reasonable person is one of the most important skills you possess. It's your responsibility to teach it to the children.

Supervising routine may be dull but it's the heart and soul of good professional child care. It's also one of the hardest skills to learn.

WAKE-UP

You may not pull wake-up duty for a while. Facilities usually prefer to use more experienced folk for this responsibility. There is a simple reason for this. Waking up a group of troubled children and giving them a good start on their day takes a high degree of skill.

Troubled children do not like to wake up. They are likely to be very unwilling to start another day. They might be downright fearful. What's to get up for, anyway?

Some workers make a basic mistake. They come on like drill sergeants. "ALL RIGHT, EVERYBODY UP!"

How would you like it if someone woke you up this way?

The best way to wake up someone is to speak in a relatively gentle tone of voice. The trick is to engage the kids in conversation and, if possible, give them a good reason to get up. A good breakfast is, of course, one of the best reasons in the world. You might mention a special activity scheduled for the day or even talk about the weather.

Pay no attention to threats not to get up. If a child says something like, "Get out of my room, I'm not getting up," you might say, "I feel the same way when I wake up. I'll be back to check on you in a few minutes."

If any children claim to be sick, check them out. They really might be sick. Even if they're not, a little sympathetic attention is probably all they're asking for.

It's usually very silly to get into a confrontation with a particular child about getting up. Five minutes after waking up is a poor time to confront anybody about anything. Most kids will get up on their own steam anyway. When the other kids get up, the reluctant will usually follow.

It really is difficult to force anyone to get up. All he or she has to do is lie there. Short of physical violence—which is absolutely wrong—there's not much you can do. Therefore, if you absolutely refuse to get into a confrontation like that, you take all the fun out of it.

There is a natural consequence you might offer in extreme cases. You might say, "Well, I'm not going to talk to you now. I'll talk to you when you're awake and what we'll talk about is how early you have to go to bed in order to be okay in the morning." That will usually do the trick. If it doesn't, you've got a serious problem on your hands and you would do well to talk to other staff members before taking action. It's likely that you have an extremely upset child on your hands and it's best to look for the cause first.

This brings up a very important point about *all* forms of supervision of children. Inexperienced workers always have the idea that any problems that occur reflect on their job performance. If a child refuses to do something, the worker is likely to feel that it's because he or she just hasn't taken the right approach. Getting that child up or showered or into bed seems like the most important thing in the world.

Children pick up on feelings like this right away. The worker is announcing, loudly and clearly, that the child is in control of the situation. That is a very unwise thing to announce.

This point bears repeating. If you can keep the proper perspective on the situation, it's the child who has the problem, not you. The minute you start thinking that it's your problem to get him or her to do what you want, you have set yourself up.

This situation can turn into something that sounds like a playground argument. "I will not." "You will too." There really is no way to force the child to conform to your wishes. The mere act of getting yourself into a confrontation undermines your authority. It's better to stay calm, offer the natural consequence ("we may decide that you need to get up earlier"), and consult other workers and your supervisor if your tactic doesn't work. This doesn't risk your authority in the slightest.

A final point—and, again, one that we will make several times—an experienced worker develops a personal style for doing things. One worker we talked to, for instance, sings people awake. Another specializes in elaborate breakfasts. Another does what can only be described as stand-up comedy. And one worker made his morning rounds with a dog trained to assist him by getting into bed with the kids and playing with them gently until they were awake. You have to find a style that's right for you.

WASHING UP

The first thing the children should do is wash up, brush their teeth, and dress in appropriate clothing for the day. If they're going to school, they should be dressed according to local standards. Clothing should be clean and in good repair. If it's a day off, the kids should be allowed to be as casual as they wish, unless there is a particular activity planned.

Direct supervision of children while they wash and dress is rarely a good idea unless the children are very young or are clearly incapable of taking care of themselves. The usual thing is to casually inspect the appearance of each child, making sure it's up to standard. This takes an eye for detail—face, nails, hair, and so on.

Some facilities place great stress on physical appearance and clothing. There is certainly good reason for such a policy. A smart appearance makes the child more proud and positive if not carried to ridiculous lengths. Knife-edge creases and shoes polished to a mirror shine are not necessary.

Physical appearance also has a lot to do with the way children are treated. Imagine what would happen if the child were to be called into the office at school. School principals are human, after all. A principal or teacher is going to make certain assumptions about a child who appears in a messy T-shirt and dirty jeans and who is otherwise unkempt, untidy, and sloppy. The fact that nearly everyone—including teachers, policemen, store owners, and the general public—jumps to conclusions is probably not fair but it still happens.

An important point: Never assume that a child knows how to do something you are asking him or her to do. Boys learn how to shave from their fathers. Girls learn about makeup and feminine hygiene from their mothers. Many children who find themselves in group care may not know everything that "everybody knows." Always ask them if they know how. If you have the slightest doubt, show them how.

One warning, though: Like a doctor or nurse, you have to be very careful about being alone in a room with a child who is undressed. You should never do this with a child of the opposite sex. You should even take sensible precautions if the child is the same sex, such as making sure that there is a witness present. This is to protect you against any allegation of sexual misconduct. Of course, beyond this element of self-protection, it is important to be sensitive to the growing child's feelings about privacy.

MAKING BEDS, AND OTHER HOUSEKEEPING TASKS

Most residences require children to make their beds and tidy up their rooms in the morning, usually before breakfast. During this period, you circulate and make sure that everyone is usefully occupied.

If a child is unusually depressed or is new to the residence, you should lend a hand; this also lets you know whether the child knows how to perform the required tasks. Children really appreciate this kind of attention. Beware, however, of giving the message that you will help every day.

Most facilities demand fairly high standards of neatness. With so many people living in the same place, high standards are necessary. If things are allowed to slide, the place will cease in short order to be a pleasant environment.

Male workers may have particular problems in this area. By and large, men are not trained to be neat. The worst thing that can happen is that male workers may leave the housekeeping tasks to female workers. This angers female workers and, really, it's a bad example for the children. Modern marriages simply don't work that way.

Certain housekeeping skills are absolutely necessary for a child care worker. You must be able to:

- make a bed
- wash clothing
- iron
- do household cleaning

How, after all, can you teach children to do these things if you don't know yourself?

Examine each child's room to be sure that the necessary tasks are completed.

BREAKFAST

Much depends, of course, on how your agency handles food. Some have cooks and institutional dining rooms. In others, child care staff members do the cooking.

Breakfast is an important meal. You use it to accomplish two things:

- you get the kids started on the right foot on the routine
- you make sure that each child gets enough nourishment to hold him or her until lunch— nutritionists tell us that an insufficient breakfast can affect behavior and school performance

If breakfast is well organized and orderly the children get a good start. If it is disorganized and disorderly, there goes your day.

If at all possible, it's a good idea to have the table set for breakfast the night before. This minimizes the effort in the morning. Setting the table is, by the way, usually one of the chores done by the children.

In most cases, staff members eat with the children and supervise them. Unlike the other meals of the day, breakfast is not an occasion to promote much conversation. Many people like to be quiet in the morning and many are irritable. Don't make too many demands.

During breakfast, as during other meals, child care workers supervise the children's table manners and eating habits. They make sure that everyone eats something and that individual children do not eat unhealthy quantities. You will encounter some children who just don't have *any* table manners. Gently, but firmly, you have to teach them.

Unfortunately, arguments and even fights are quick to break out in the morning. If two children start an argument, react to it before it spreads. (This is a policy you should follow any time—day or night, weekday or weekend, inside or out-of-doors.) If there is a real issue involved in the argument, one staff member should deal with the children involved away from the group. In many cases, such arguments are pure irritability, or nervousness about school, family visits, and similar things.

SEEING THEM OFF

In most cases the children then begin their day program, usually school. As mentioned earlier, some agencies have on-ground schools and others don't. In *either* case, the residential staff should make absolutely sure to maintain good relationships and open communications with school authorities.

Like the proverbial customer, the school (or the neighbor) is always right. If you work with school personnel, give them a courteous hearing and quick service and your agency will be very pleased with you. More on neighbors later.

The teachers' most frequent problem is dealing with children who have arrived at school improperly equipped or prepared. Child care workers should keep track of books and gym bags and make sure that the children don't leave them at home. The best method is to check the kids out one at a time, making sure that they have everything they need. Don't forget lunches, or lunch money for those who need it. Papers from the school requiring signatures should be promptly returned.

Facilities using schools in the community do periodic attendance checks and call frequently just to find out how things are going.

LUNCH

You may or may not have children home for lunch. In some residences, especially those with on-grounds schools, you may have the whole crew.

In any case, lunch is the least formal meal of the day. Children usually like to sit and talk to their friends or sit by themselves and think. This calls for a *somewhat* relaxed approach to supervision, in most cases. You should intervene only if it's absolutely necessary. You should give the kids space to be with each other or by themselves. You can, of course, spend time with any child who seems to be having difficulty.

There is a kind of relaxed supervision called "listening with one ear." It takes time to perfect. After a while on the job, you will be able to sit and talk with one child and automatically listen for a discordant note in the rest of the room. You will be able to separate a developing fight from the background noise in a matter of seconds—before anything actually occurs. This is an ideal form of supervision for lunchtime.

HOME FROM SCHOOL

As you checked out each child individually, check each in individually. First of all and above all else, make sure that everyone is accounted for. Ask each child how he or she is doing and how the day went at school.

An experienced child care worker remarks, "I let the kids know that as long as they tell me the truth and tell me in advance, before the school or somebody else calls to tell me, I'll always try to help. They know that if they don't tell me, one of the things we'll have to talk about is that they didn't tell me. The kids learn pretty soon that not telling me only adds to their problem. After a while, they'll hurry to be the first one to tell the story."

Many experienced child care workers are absolutely experts at detecting when a child is telling the truth and when he or she isn't.

The same worker continues, "I tell them that I'm a simpleminded person; I believe what I'm told until I find out different. If I find out that you're lying to me once, I'll have to check out everything you say to me in the future. That won't be much fun and it will be a while before I take your word for anything again. You'll have to work on regaining my trust. I not only say that; that's what I do. In the end I make it easier to tell me the truth." Generally, adults—not just children—pick up on that.

There are, as well, positive reasons for asking children how their schoolday went. Children like to talk about it. It's a chance to blow off steam about their teachers or talk about the perfect score they got in spelling.

When the initial rush is over, afterschool is usually a quiet time. The children play games, listen to music, or watch television. It's a good time for the worker to spend special time with individuals.

DINNER

This is, without doubt, the most important time of the day. What happens around the dinner table says all that need be said about any living group, whether family or facility.

For some reason, and it probably goes back to early human history, sharing dinner is a powerful expression of togetherness. This does not mean that it is always positive. For some families and some children in facilities, and on some occasions, dinner can at times feel chaotic. If one puts a group of persons who aren't sure that they want to be together around a dinner table, a great deal of anxiety can result.

Much depends, again, on how the residence handles food. We feel, however, that dinner should be a relatively formal occasion. You shouldn't just pile into the dining room and eat. The group, staff and children, should eat together in much the same way as a family does. You don't begin until everyone is served and you sit until everyone is finished. Dinner table conversation, with only one person speaking at a time, should be encouraged.

Every now and then, it's a good idea to hold a fancy dinner. Use a tablecloth and put candles on

the table. Everyone has to get dressed up. The
kids love it.

Dinner, or after dinner, is the time for announce-
ments or general statements.

CHORES

Most residences require the children to do regular chores and a list of regular chores is usually
posted. Children rotate from one job to another
on a weekly and daily basis. Some of these lists
sound like a railroad time table. Most are relatively
simple.

There is usually, as well, a complete description
of what each chore involves. You should study
these descriptions carefully. Disputes over who is
supposed to do what are common. The children
will argue, for example, whether the person washing dishes must also take them out of the rinse
water or whether this is a responsibility of the person drying. At times you will feel like a judge sitting
on a complicated antitrust case.

Another frequent occurrence is absolute refusal. "I'm not going to wash your (obscenity
deleted) dishes." Once again, it is important not to
get sucked into the no-I-won't—yes-you-will game.
It goes nowhere and it's loud. Beyond that, residences have different ways of handling refusal.
The most frequent is the revocation of privileges
until the child is willing to accept his or her
responsibilities.

One experienced worker has often used a novel
method. She believes that refusal to do chores is
usually just a means of starting an argument and

legitimizing an expression of anger that probably comes from some other source. The child wants the staff member to get mad so that he or she can get mad in return. When the child refuses to do a chore, the worker sometimes says, "I'm not going to argue with you. I'll give you a few minutes to get started. If you don't, I'll do it myself. Then we'll talk about what's really bothering you unless you want to talk about it now. I'm afraid that we'll also have to talk about what you'll have to do to make up for your chore." She claims that this often works. The child usually does the chore and talks about what the trouble really is.

Another good way to get chores done quickly and well is to make them fun. One worker has made up a series of "work songs for dishwashing and vacuuming." She gets the children singing things like "Jump down, run around, wash a load of dishes."

Children like to have staff members work with them. If you make a practice out of bustling around simultaneously supervising the kids and doing a few chores yourself, you will get better performance from them. Keep your standards high. If you think that the child can do a better job, insist that he or she do so. Once again, make absolutely certain that the child knows how.

Check all the chores before beginning any other activity.

EVENING

Some nights will be taken up with special activities and meetings. Since these are dealt with in later chapters, we will discuss the ordinary evening at home here.

Homework

Most residences have a "quiet hour" either before or after dinner. During this time children must be engaged in homework or in other quiet activities. Staff members usually help children with homework during this hour.

Television

Like other kids, children in residential facilities watch a fair amount of television. If you don't already believe that television is an invention of the devil, you soon will.

The television causes more fights and arguments than any other single thing. The usual argument is over what to watch. After you've heard a few hundred hours of heated discussions of the relative merits of reruns of "Star Trek" and reruns of "M*A*S*H," you'll be ready to resort to Solomon's solution and split the television set in half.

The usual rule is that the majority of people actually in the room at the time decides. In the event of a tie, a coin is tossed. If there is an excessively violent argument, the staff turns off the set for the evening. But even this isn't foolproof. Some devious soul may pack the house with friends who vote for his or her selection and then promptly leave. The minority may wait until someone has gone to answer the telephone or to the bathroom and then treacherously demand a vote. It *never* ends.

Games

Most children are avid game players. If the residence has a reasonable selection of games, the children are likely to spend a lot of time with them. They especially like to have a staff member in the game. This is a good way to establish relationships with the kids.

Conversation

Conversation is one of the best activities, particularly if it is on subjects important to the children. The child care worker should make certain that there are opportunities for meaningful conversation.

Baths

Children usually are allowed to bathe as frequently as they wish. At some facilities there are bath nights for particular children (usually every other day) to make sure that they take regular baths. If this is the case, there will be a written schedule. On any given night, you round up the children on the list and make sure that they take their baths. (Be warned: the old Tom Sawyer trick of wetting the hair and coming out of the bathroom with a towel around the neck is not unknown.)

Supervision

While all of these diverse activities are going on, you have to keep tabs on everyone, even if you're involved in one of the activities. If children are allowed to leave the unit, you must know where they are going and when they will be back. They should give you this information before they leave.

In open residences, violations of the curfew hours are frequent. Children will, in particular, test a new staff member to see if he or she will allow them to be late. And, of course, if you let them be late, they will try being later. It's a good idea to get a reputation for placing importance on punctuality.

Lateness may result in a number of consequences, depending on the residence. It may mean losing "points" and privileges. Many facilities require the child to come in correspondingly early on the next night. A person who is habitually late may be "grounded" for a night.

You must, by the way, keep close track of "grounded" children. One of them may approach you and ask if he or she can go out. If you are unaware of the "grounding" you may give permission. Later the argument will be, "Well he (she) told me I could!"

As the children return, check them out. Look for signs of drug or alcohol use. This is, unfortunately, widespread. In most communities it is virtually impossible to isolate children from drugs. Open facilities have continuing problems with substance abuse among residents. All you can do is keep a careful eye on children when they return.

Agencies handle drug involvement in many different ways. Most "ground" the child, at a minimum.

BEDTIME

As bedtime approaches, the child care staff starts getting everyone in a quiet mood. All loud or vigorous activities are wound up. One worker told us that she actually goes around turning off some of the lights.

It's rare for all the children to go to bed at the same time. This is fortunate because it is not easy to get everyone properly quiet and relaxed for sleep at the same time. Bedtimes are usually graduated according to age and sometimes according to status within the facility. That is, children who have successfully completed a stage of the program are given a later bedtime.

It is excellent practice for a staff member to spend 15 minutes or so with each child, reading or telling a story, giving a backrub, or just quietly talking, depending on the age and preference of the child. Troubled children have a hard time going to sleep. Spending time with them makes it easier.

WEEKEND ROUTINE

Contacts between children and their families are vital in dealing, over time, with the problems that brought the children to the residence in the first place. More about this later.

The weekend is the obvious and usual time for children and their families to see each other. Agencies differ in their visiting practices. Some typically have parents visit at the residence. Others typically send children to their own homes. Some do both. In still others, parents also participate in on-grounds activities with the children. What is certain is that the child care worker is a key person in all these contacts.

The following represents some common visiting patterns.

Friday (or Saturday morning) is a hard time in most residential facilities. This is when children start weekend visits to their families or await their families at the residence. One should expect lots of excitement, not a little anxiety, and plenty of old-fashioned confusion.

You cannot send a child home or have a family visit at the residence unless arrangements have been made in advance. The family may pick up the child at a specified hour or the staff may drop the child off at the family home. Older, more responsible children use public transportation. If the wires get crossed and a child who expects to visit doesn't, or be visited isn't, you are going to have a very upset child on your hands.

Many children are anxious about visits. For this reason you will note that you have more problems than usual as the time approaches. If a child gets into trouble, it may be that he or she is trying, consciously or unconsciously, to get the visit canceled and relieve the anxiety. Bear this in mind when you deal with the child.

Going Out

If you work in an open facility from which children are permitted to go out, some weekend periods can be harrowing. Alcohol or drug use is a definite possibility.

If you suspect that a child is drunk or under the influence of drugs, do *not* confront him or her at the time. If at all possible, put the child to bed and keep a careful eye on his or her physical condition for the rest of the night. Talk to the child on the following morning or pass the information on to the next shift. There is *no* point whatever in trying to talk to a person who is drunk or under the influence of drugs. It's very likely, after all, that the child would have no recollection of anything you said. It's also likely that his or her reaction to confrontation would be extremely hostile.

Never forget that drugs and alcohol, particularly in combination, can kill. Monitor the child's physical condition carefully and get medical help if you have any reason to believe that the child is ill. If you are concerned, try to find out immediately what the child has been taking and in what quantities. The doctor will need to know this. Large quantities of alcohol or combinations of alcohol and "downers" (tranquilizers, sleeping pills, etc.) are particularly dangerous.

Relaxation

Weekend calls for a relaxation in the routine. Children are usually allowed to sleep late and responsibilities are taken at a more leisurely pace.

There will frequently be a special activity, and if
there isn't, you can put together a game of softball,
or some suitable indoor activity.

Sunday

Religious practices in agencies differ. Some facilities have their own on-grounds religious services.
Others use local churches. Some use both.

Most agencies have no exclusive religious orientation, including many with sectarian names, and
accept children of different religions. They usually
send the children to the churches attended by
their families. In practice, few facilities are willing
to exert much pressure on the child to attend
although they certainly encourage the child to do
so. Staff members usually accompany children to
services.

Agencies with a single, exclusive religious orientation discuss this with families in advance. These
facilities accept only those children whose parents
wish them to attend the particular religious services offered. Attendance at such services is usually required.

You must be wary of trying to sway children
toward your religion although you certainly have a
constitutional right to express your religious opinions. The family, however, also has traditional
rights concerning the religious education of their
children. This is one of those gray areas where it is
difficult to sort out the rights and wrongs. As a
professional child care worker, it is your responsibility to consider the feelings of the child's family.

When children return from home visits, you should check out each child carefully. Look for signs of emotional upset or substance abuse. Ask each one how it went. Don't forget to count them. Sunday night is a prime time for runaways.

EXCEPTIONS TO THE ROUTINE

Appointments

The children will have frequent appointments with doctors, dentists, social workers, psychologists, and other professionals. There is *only* one way to make sure that none are missed: PUT ALL APPOINTMENTS IN WRITING! Keep an appointment calendar listing *all* appointments for the children. If your agency doesn't already do this, make one up. It pays off.

Remind children of appointments. Make sure transportation is arranged. Find out how each child feels about the appointment. Make sure he or she is to be accompanied if it seems necessary. Some people are terrified of dentists. Others feel the same way about psychologists! Take the child's feelings into account.

A.W.O.L.

Your facility will have a routine for handling runaways. It will tell you what to do and whom to call. Make yourself thoroughly familiar with it.

The essence of a runaway report is the physical description. The police will request a complete description, including clothing. Many agencies keep a "runaway file" with all the relevant information, except, of course, what the child is wearing. If your agency doesn't, it would be a good idea to suggest keeping a file if running away occurs frequently.

Experienced child care workers note what a child is wearing automatically before allowing him or her to leave the premises. If you don't trust your memory, write down a description of the child's appearance.

Restrictions

Most agencies restrict children's privileges for a variety of reasons. Put any restrictions you make in writing. Carefully note any restrictions already applied and carry them out.

There is no quicker way to become unpopular with other staff members than to fail to carry out a restriction. They will feel that you are undermining their authority. If you feel that they aren't being fair, talk to *them* about it, not to the child.

Be fair in your own restrictions. Apply as few as possible and only when the child actually needs the restriction.

Don't let your anger influence your decisions. Always listen to what the child has to say. Remember that you probably won't be the one who has to enforce the restriction. Staff members also don't like people who give out excessive, numerous, or frivolous restrictions.

Excuses

It seems only right to end a chapter about the routine with a few comments about excuses.

Where there is routine, there are excuses. You will hear that the bus had a flat tire, that the clock at school stopped and, possibly, that the child stopped to save a drowning puppy (this also explains the wet clothing). You will also hear about strange (and sudden) allergies to dishwater, windowpanes that break spontaneously, and teachers who announce school holidays that don't exist. At times, against your will, you will find yourself smiling.

You have to exercise a little tolerant adult judgment, bearing in mind that strange and unlikely things can happen. Accepting too many excuses, though, would bring the routine grinding to a halt. You have to be fair but firm.

6

Child Management

Child management is another important child care skill. It involves building positive relationships with children and carrying out your agency's program of treatment. Acceptable child management varies from agency to agency, depending on the program offered. Much of child management is nothing more than sensible, caring adult behavior toward children. You *cannot* master child management until you have mastered the routine.

Reading this chapter will not teach you child management. There is no substitute for on-the-job training and child care courses at a university or college. We hope, merely, to acquaint you with some of the issues and, in keeping with the rest of this book, the practical aspects. Child management training is readily available from many sources. We hope that you will seek out one of these sources.

CHILD CARE AND SERVICE PLANNING

Service planning is the process of deciding what help a child needs and how to deliver the appropriate services. It starts with a complete assessment of each child and an individual plan for him or her. Child care workers may participate in this process by discussing their experiences with the child and, of course, by carrying out their part of the service plan.

Assessment

Assessment may include any of the following items. Many are provided by the agency referring the child to the residential facility:

- psychological tests
- psychiatric diagnosis
- medical reports
- social history (family background, early history, etc.)
- educational report and tests
- reports from people who have worked with the child
- reports from the child care staff (if the child has been at the facility long enough)

Assessment does not necessarily include all of these items. What the assessment includes depends on the type of facility.

Establishing Needs

On the basis of information available about the child, a planning team discusses what the child

needs. In many facilities child care staff members
are on the planning team.

Setting Goals

The team then establishes overall goals for the
child on the basis of those needs. A goal might be
something like "Johnny will develop better relationships with other children."

Objectives

The team breaks down the goals into a specific
set of reasonable objectives that the team believes
the child will be able to meet in a specific time
period. If Johnny needs to develop better relationships with peers, the objectives might be "Within
six months Johnny will stop getting into provoked
fights with other residents," or, "Within three
months Johnny will begin to participate at group
meetings."

Methodology

The team works out how the objectives will be
met, listing the techniques to be used and suggested approaches to the child's behavior.

Implementation

The team will usually assign personnel to be
responsible for specific tasks.

Evaluation

The team may also decide how to determine if
the goals and objectives are met.

You and the Service Plan

The service planning process varies from facility to facility. Some do not draw up written plans, although this is definitely the wave of the future.

You should be familiar with each child's service plan and tailor your approaches accordingly. You should be especially aware of any features of the plan to be carried out by the child care staff.

THE RULES

Most facilities have written rules for children's behavior. These rules are usually few and simple.

One agency director remarks, "These are the rules we use: no drugs or stuff used with drugs; no sex with other residents; be on time when you're expected to be somewhere; no violence or threats of violence. The last and most important rule is: don't stick peanuts up your nose. By that we mean that the kids shouldn't do anything that doesn't make good sense even if there's no rule against it."

This simple set of rules is fairly typical. One of the basic laws of child care is, "Never make a rule you can't enforce." There is a real difference between saying "Never swear" and "Don't swear in front of me." If a worker tells a child never to swear, the worker has made a rule that cannot be enforced. The child can go off out of earshot, swear like a trooper, and feel that he or she has really put one over on the worker.

A rule that can be easily broken or broken without consequences teaches disrespect for the rest of the rules.

Most facilities also avoid excessively harsh rules and rules with fixed penalties. If, for instance, you were to say, "Anyone who uses drugs will be grounded for a *week*," you are locked in, no matter what the circumstances. You can't take the child's past behavior into account or look at the reasons for drug use. Worse than that, what has a child who has already been grounded for a week got to lose? Good behavior won't help him or her and bad behavior won't hurt. A week is an impossibly long period for most children.

Some prefer to base the duration of consequences on behavior. They will ground a child until further notice—that is, until the child demonstrates that he or she can be trusted.

In many facilities the children as a group participate in determining the consequences for a particular child. This system can work only if properly supervised by staff because children tend to be much more severe than adults on infractions of the rules.

One important point: no system works unless staff members are relatively consistent about how they handle things. As an employee of the agency, it is your responsibility to carry out agency policy. If you don't like the rules, the proper thing to do is to speak up at a staff meeting. Disregarding the rules you don't like is damaging to the program and will probably get the other staff members angry at you.

Consequences

You will probably be involved in establishing consequences for infractions of the rules. You may, depending on the program, be required to administer consequences more or less independently.

Many facilities favor the idea of "natural consequence." A natural consequence is precisely that —a consequence, not a punishment.

Let's try to explain the difference between a consequence and a punishment. When you punish someone, you are saying to them, in effect, "if you do thus and such, I am going to do something unpleasant to you." The idea of punishment is not only particularly inhumane, it isn't all that effective either. In your career of working with troubled children, you will meet many who have been punished horribly all their lives. You will find that there is really very little that you would be willing to do that would come close to matching what others have done to them. Hurting people is a poor way to teach them, unless you are trying to teach them that powerful people have a legitimate right to force their will on the powerless.

A natural consequence is exactly what it sounds like. It is a consequence closely linked to the action the child has committed. In some cases it means the child righting a wrong, like repaying stolen money. In other cases it may mean the staff assuming closer supervision of a child who is unable to make wise decisions about his or her own behavior. A child who has committed a dangerous act in the community might be restricted to the residence. A child who gets into constant trouble with peers might be placed under constant staff supervision. One facility sometimes requires such a child to hold hands with a staff member at all times. This is not designed to humiliate the child; it is a radical measure designed to ensure *complete* safety for the child.

One of the better aspects of the idea of natural consequence is that it can also be applied to positive behavior. If a child does something that demonstrates responsibility, greater trust will be placed in him or her. Any good system of child management provides rewards for positive behavior as well as negative consequences for undesirable behavior.

POINTS

There are a number of types of "point" systems. They all boil down to the same principle. A child can earn points for positive behavior and lose points for negative behavior. Points can be exchanged for certain privileges, rewards, or, sometimes, allowance money.

If your agency uses a point system, you will be trained in how to score different behaviors.

SUPPORTIVE COUNSELING

This is what most people imagine themselves doing when they become child care workers. Supportive counseling involves building relationships with the children and helping them learn to solve problems.

The mistake most new workers make is going too far too fast with a child. Before you can begin to build a supportive counseling relationship with a child, you must gain his or her trust.

The routine in its finest form is one of the most effective ways of expressing caring and building trust that we know of. The routine, you might say, speaks louder than words. What it says to the child is that the worker is there to provide food, clothing, shelter, safety, protection, supervision, recreation, and all the other things that go into nurturance. And on a twenty-four-hour, seven-day-a-week basis. If you concentrate on the routine, the child will come to trust, like, and, possibly, love you. Then, of course, it will be easy to talk to him or her.

There is no great mystery in supportive counseling. Most of it is plain common sense. It is certainly *not* the same kind of counseling psychologists and psychiatrists do. In fact, you must be wary of falling into the trap of becoming a junior psychologist and performing "therapy."

Listening

Supportive counseling is ninety percent listening and trying to understand. Unfortunately, as has been observed often, few people know how to listen.

The first rule is, of course, that you can't listen while you're talking. If you become a good listener, you will discover an amazing and little-known fact about people. Most of them are dying to talk to somebody. In fact, the listening habit will radically change your social life. Just by listening, you will discover, you have suddenly become a nice, sympathetic person. Other people are drawn to a listener.

Try this experiment. The next time friends engage you in conversation, try listening to them carefully. Keep nodding your head and making little sounds to let them know that you're with them. If they pause, ask a question, like "Well, how did you feel about that?" Or, "What are you going to do?" If they ask you a question, say something, like "I don't know, what do you think?"

You will probably notice something interesting. First of all, it's unlikely that your friend will notice that you aren't contributing to the conversation. Second, the other person will gladly fill up the space you're leaving vacant and will respond positively to your paying such careful attention to what he or she is saying. This is really rather ironic, if you consider that most of us spend a lot of time worrying about what we're saying and what kind of impression we're making. In fact, the best way to make a favorable impression on anybody is to listen to them.

One experienced worker says, "It's very strange. Over the years I've developed the habit of sympathetic listening and now I can't turn it off on my free time. People seek me out to talk to me and tell me the most intimate things about themselves. If you listen, you get the impression that there aren't many other people who do. I'm not complaining though. I've learned a lot."

Understanding

It is not enough, of course, merely to listen. You have to try to understand, and this is difficult.

Who are you? What kind of neighborhood did you grow up in? What's your ethnic background? What kind of family raised you? These are only some of the questions whose answers affect your ability to understand the children you work with.

All human beings have set ideas based on their previous experience. Although we often think of fixed ideas as a bad thing, many are useful tools that keep us from having to examine every new situation in detail. An example: Based on our previous experience, we assume that if we turn the little round knob, the door will open. We don't have to think about it. If we did, our progress through the world would be slowed considerably.

The point is that we can't help forming set ideas—it's how our minds work. But fixed ideas about people can become prejudices if ideas are applied across the board. People are not like doors. Each human being is a unique individual with a unique set of experiences. Judging people on the basis of race, religion, sex, or national origin does not promote understanding; it blinds us.

And yet, *everyone* has some prejudices about other people. A person who denies ever having felt prejudice against certain classes of people—black people, white people, Hispanics, Jews, Asians, women, men, Catholics, Protestants, and so on— is self-deceiving. The *only* way to defeat this kind of prejudice in yourself is to examine it honestly.

In fact, people from all these backgrounds have more in common with each other than they think. The mythical man from Mars would probably have difficulty telling us apart. One worker says, "Who was it who said they never met a man they didn't like? Will Rogers. I can't say that myself. I can say this, though. After all these years working with people, I have never met anyone who has done anything that I can't imagine doing, under certain circumstances. I can imagine sleeping in cars, stealing, becoming a drug addict, wanting to hurt other people, even killing. I can understand being crazy. When I first realized this, it scared me beyond belief. Now I think it just makes me a member of the human race."

Understanding someone else's social background is certainly very difficult. If, as a child, you never experienced cold, hunger, poverty, neglect, or physical abuse it may be very difficult for you to understand many of the children who live in residential facilities. It may be even more difficult for you to understand their parents who, as children, generally experienced the same conditions. You may end up, as many do, sympathizing with the children but not with their parents.

It's natural and very human to want to find someone to blame for the evils of the world. If you really begin to understand people, though, it becomes harder and harder to do.

There may be some pitfalls, however, in understanding *too well* the social background of your client. One pitfall is to believe that since you turned out OK, the child will be OK if left alone. Being "left alone" means not exerting any limits on the child's behavior, not enforcing natural consequences, accepting lame excuses for unacceptable behavior, and so forth. A child who does not experience your firmness along with your understanding will not perceive your lack of limits as love and understanding. He or she will perceive it as rejection and assume that you don't care.

Another pitfall in working with children who have essentially the same background as you do is that you can be very judgmental about the child and/or his or her parents. "When I was growing up," you'll pontificate, "We were very poor, but we didn't behave like you hoodlums!" Or, "I raised six children by myself after my husband died, and I never went on welfare, and I never put any of my children into a home." Remember, no matter how similar your background may be, there have been some differences, and nobody elected you judge of us all!

Repeating You can *never* be sure that any person means the same things by the words he or she is using that you understand them to mean. The only way to be sure is to repeat what the person seems to be saying in your own words. Repeating is useful in more ways than one. Not only does it ensure that you really are understanding what the person is saying, it also gives the person a chance to listen to himself or herself. Not only do people not listen to others, they also don't listen to themselves. Repeating stimulates thought and self-examination.

To keep the person talking, it is best to frame repetitions in the form of a question, like "Let me see, are you saying that . . . ?"

Sensible Advice and Help

Workers who get into a "junior psychologist" role often take the position that you should never give your children advice, merely assist them in solving their problems. Our advice is to leave professional counseling to professional counselors.

In living with children on a day-to-day basis, a child care worker develops an entirely different kind of relationship with them than does the professional counselor. The child care worker's role is broadly similar to parenting. Common-sense advice is certainly a part of good parenting.

At some point in a supportive counseling relationship, you must ask yourself what you can do to help the child solve his or her problems. You must also ask the child and work out a reasonable plan between you.

As a child care worker, you should never forget your role as a link between the child and the resources available through your facility. In talking with children you will encounter many problems that you just are not equipped to handle. It's your job to get the child to the service he or she needs. You are a friend, adviser, and responsible adult, but you are not a psychologist, psychiatrist, social worker, or medical doctor. You are also not working alone and should not make plans for a particular child independent of your team.

The Supportive Relationship

You will find that it is not possible to develop a supportive counseling relationship with every child. Some children will take to you and others won't. There are many factors affecting a child's trust or distrust of you that are totally beyond your control. You may, for instance, be similar in appearance to someone who has mistreated the child. The child may have difficulties relating to persons of your sex or race. The child may not share your interests. Though many of these things eventually may be overcome, it may be impossible for you and the child really to be close.

If the child obviously has a hard time dealing with you, don't push it. In fact, avoid any but routine dealings with the child. If it appears to you that the child is having a problem, clue in a worker who seems to have a better relationship with the child, unless, of course, you're alone and the problem just won't wait.

If your relationship with a particular child becomes too strained, sit down with the child and a worker the child trusts and talk it over, if your team agrees that this is desirable. Tell the child that he or she doesn't have to be your friend, that you are just looking for a way to get along.

The Dividing Line

You will frequently hear colleagues describing a fellow worker as "overinvolved" with a child—meaning that the worker is so emotionally tied in with a child that he or she can no longer be objective.

Many workers take this to mean that you cannot become emotionally involved, and this, let us say without hesitation, is ridiculous. A child care worker who does not get emotionally involved with children is in the wrong work.

Overinvolvement is just the wrong kind of involvement. You have to be able to separate yourself and your problems from the child and his or her problems at all times. You can't let the child's problems become your problems.

Be careful not to succumb to the temptation of trying to have your needs met through your clients. Be sure that you have a life away from the job whether you are a live-in worker or a shift worker. Don't begin to see yourself as being so essential to the life of your client(s) that you don't take your days off, or you can't dream of using up your vacation days. When you go to this extreme, you are not being supportive of your clients, you are trying to extract solutions for your unmet needs from your job. Assuming someone else's problems as your own is never a favor to them. It doesn't help in the slightest.

The only way to make sure that your relationship with a child is appropriate is to check it out with others. Ask the other people on the team what they think.

CRISIS MANAGEMENT

Crisis management is a series of techniques to use when a child is in crisis. What is a crisis? Broadly, it's when people become so upset or angry that they're a clear threat to the safety of themselves or other people. Crisis management is designed to keep the breakage of people and property to an absolute minimum.

WARNING! You cannot learn crisis management from this book or any other book. A person experienced in crisis management can teach you

through role playing sessions and demonstrations.
Do not attempt any use of physical restraint without training.

What To Do

As an inexperienced worker you should not attempt to deal with a child in crisis if there is a more
experienced person available. Ask the more experienced worker if he or she requires assistance. Do
exactly what the experienced worker tells you to
do.

The first step usually is to remove all bystanders
from the room. Attempting to remove any of the
children involved in the situation will probably
start a fight. Don't do so unless instructed.
Someone—probably you—should be with the other
children, keeping them calm and *away* from the
immediate area of the crisis.

There should be at least two staff members
present in the crisis area. One does the actual
handling. The other takes a position in the background and observes. He or she may actually sit
down to reduce the threat to the child. This
worker should be positioned, however, to block
the child's exit and the entrance of other children.
(It's not a bad idea to sit down on the floor physi-
cally obstructing the door.) This worker does not
make a move unless requested to do so by the
worker dealing with the child.

There are several preferred methods for the
worker dealing with the crisis. Most prefer to
stand in a relaxed position just beyond the child's
reach with a blow or a kick. Some workers clasp

their arms across the front of their chests to have the hands in position to block a blow or kick. The idea, of course, is to avoid getting to that stage.

The trick is to keep the child talking. As long as he or she is talking, the less chance there is of violence. The longer the child talks, the harder it will be for him or her to work up the energy to attack or run. Anger works on the body instantly. There is a rush of blood and energy. The body is in an unnatural state of alertness. The body cannot maintain this state for very long. If you keep the person talking, the moment of readiness eases.

It is absolutely imperative that the staff members present keep relaxed. The staff member dealing with the child should speak in a calm voice and make no sudden moves. This worker should keep reassuring the child that he or she will not be hurt. Keep the child responding—usually by asking questions. It is also important not to back the child into a corner. The worker usually tells the child that all he or she has to do is keep talking.

Practically speaking, you may encounter crises before you gain the proper experience. If training is not provided to you, ask your supervisor or an experienced worker to instruct you.

Passive Physical Restraint   Passive physical restraint techniques are methods for restraining or "holding" a child in a way that doesn't hurt. They are applied *only* when there is no other way to keep the child from violence.

Some older workers use holds taught by the police, generally called "come-alongs." Before the development of passive physical restraint, the use of come-alongs was widespread. Most come-along holds hurt. Never use any hold shown to you by another worker unless it is totally painless.

Passive physical restraint techniques are "holds" in the strictest sense. They involve "holding" the child without applying painful pressure. In short, you exert your strength merely to keep the child from moving, not against any part of the child's body.

One of the most approved methods is called the "Browndale." The worker is seated directly behind the child and in complete contact with the child's body. The worker holds the child's wrists. The child's arms are crossed across his or her chest. The worker merely holds the arms in this position without exerting pressure. The worker's legs are hooked around the child's body over the top of the child's legs, again without exerting painful pressure. Ideally, the worker's back is to a wall.

Do not attempt this hold without expert supervision. We describe it merely to make a point. The Browndale and most other passive restraint techniques we are aware of have one thing in common. They involve considerable physical contact—they are almost like embraces. A person who is embarrassed about making physical contact with others will have a problem with these techniques.

Likening passive physical restraint to an embrace is a comparison in more ways than one. Experienced people will tell you that it can be a very caring thing to do for a child. The message, ultimately, is that you are prepared to go to considerable lengths to protect the child. For the child, a holding is frequently an experience of emotional catharsis. It is a chance to rant, rave, and release all the pent-up anger and frustration in perfect safety. There is a real possibility that some children will go into crisis just to be held.

Whatever the situation, passive physical restraint is not a technique to be used lightly or frequently. Ultimately, a "holding," as some call it, is a radical deprivation of a child's freedom of choice. It may in some cases be applied because the worker is angry and unsure of his or her own control—and this is wrong. In some agencies, "holding," like other new techniques in the field, becomes a panacea, a common response to a child with a problem. That, too, is wrong. Physical restraint does not teach problem solving. It is, in fact, a tacit admission of the immediate failure of other methods.

ABUSE AND NEGLECT

Child abuse and neglect have recently received a lot of attention in the press. They represent serious problems for our society.

Abuse and neglect occur at residential facilities, too. Considering the thousands of hours of good child care provided, the incidence is rare but it does happen.

Abuse and neglect are against the law. As a citizen you are required to report any incident of abuse or neglect to the authorities. You can get into serious trouble for failing to report. Your supervisor will no doubt acquaint you with the state law on the subject. There are variations from state to state on the definitions of abuse and neglect, to whom they have to be reported, and the penalties.

There is a simple way to avoid being guilty of abuse. Never do anything intended to hurt, humiliate, or even frighten a child. Why would you want to do any of these things, anyway?

There is an equally simple way to avoid being guilty of neglect. Follow the routine. Take good care of the children. See that they are properly fed, clothed, sheltered, and supervised. Make sure that they're healthy. That's your job.

Notice that we said that you can avoid being *guilty* of abuse or neglect. We can't promise you that, in your long and glorious career, someone isn't going, for one reason or another, to accuse you of abuse or neglect. We can promise you that the law protects you, too. A complete investigation will be done and, if you are indeed innocent, you have nothing to worry about. This is true despite whatever dark, underground rumors you may hear to the contrary. If anybody tells you differently, ask him or her to name *one* worker who was totally innocent who got into trouble as the result of such charges.

7

Activities
and Leisure

Child care staff members are always taxing their brains for activities that the children enjoy. This chapter is a grab-bag of programming ideas.

The essence of putting together a successful activity is planning and organization. Spontaneity is okay, but before you get the kids excited about doing something, make sure that you have adequate funds and transportation. Check to make sure that the proposed activity is available. (Don't put together a trip to the zoo, only to find that it isn't open for another month.) Collect the necessary equipment and check it to see that it's in good condition. (Being in a rainstorm in a tent that leaks like a sieve with eight wet and unhappy kids can only be described as punishing.)

Always plan for the worst. Have an alternative ready if it rains, if the snow melts, or if the car won't start.

USING YOUR HEAD

Planning activities for children isn't hard if you use some imagination. You will find that the kids can get interested in anything if you have a good approach.

Your own interests are good tools in selecting activities. If you're athletic-minded, organize some sports. If you have a hobby, get the kids involved. Teaching them to like something you like is that much easier.

In any activity you choose, you have to take an adult supervisory role. It's okay to play with the kids but you have to remember that the whole point is for *them to relax and learn*. They won't learn much from watching you hot-dog around the court racking up an astronomical score for your team. They won't enjoy watching you building their go-cart or sewing their new shirt, either. You have to teach them and keep them involved. You have to avoid competing with them.

Competing in any activity makes it harder to handle. Many children just can't compete without getting upset or angry. The school of thought that says that competition is always "healthy" may be okay for professional football teams but it doesn't have any place in recreational activities for troubled children. On the whole, fun and exercise should be stressed more than winning the game.

You should avoid sexual stereotypes in devising activities. Some girls like to engage in sports. Some boys like cooking and macrame. What's wrong with that?

WARMING UP THE CROWD

It is hard to get a group of children to agree on the time of day. No matter what activity you come up with, some children are going to tell you that they don't want to go. That doesn't mean that they don't really want to go, though, of course, you can't always make this assumption. Some children rebel against group activities as a means of getting attention. Others do it because they're angry. Some are seeking rejection from the group, usually because they think that the group will reject them, anyway.

You don't just come out and say, "Do you guys want to go camping next weekend?" That's asking for trouble.

One night, around the dinner table, you say, "You know, I haven't been camping this year. Last year I went up to Sawtooth National Park. We had a campsite right on the lake. We got up every morning and jumped in the water." Pretty soon you're hearing about every camping trip every one of the kids or their Uncle Ed ever went on. Very likely, that's all you have to do. Sooner or later, someone is bound to say, "Hey, I've got an idea. Why can't we go on a camping trip?" Then, if you're really cunning, you might say, "Well, I don't know. It's kind of a long drive and we would have to get all the equipment ready and everything. I guess I might be willing to do it if you really want to."

If nobody speaks up, you can casually mention the idea yourself.

Some people use the alternative method of sheer unbridled infectious enthusiasm. This works, too, if it suits your personality.

Another alternative is to take suggestions from the group. Children have some wonderful ideas for activities and like to participate in such decisions. One worker once took a group of children to the airport to watch the planes take off. Everyone had hot dogs on the observation deck and got an impromptu talk from a passing pilot (one of the kids asked him a question about an airplane). They loved it. But until one of the group suggested this activity, it never occurred to this child care worker that none of the children had ever been in an airport. On another occasion they toured a local fast-food franchise, again at a child's suggestion. It turned out that that particular company has regular tours.

FREEBIES

Money is *always* a problem. Fortunately, there are many free fun activities. It's amazing how many companies and public agencies give guided tours. Even the waterworks will show you around.

A little scouting of schools and recreation centers will probably turn up a swimming pool or gymnasium that you can use. It's a good idea to have a list of the possibilities.

And, of course, you can always get a game together if you have the equipment.

There are civic groups that give away free tickets to different events. Commercial shows, like circuses, ice shows, and concerts, can be prevailed upon.

Some workers have a talent for getting freebies. It takes nerve and a good telephone voice. One worker we know is famous for her triumphs, the greatest of which was getting a free full-course meal at *the* Chinese restaurant in her area.

If all else fails, children like to "just drive around." Somehow sitting in a car seems to relax them—after an initial period of noise. You can drive around for a while, buy ice cream cones, and watch the sunset. The only problem can be the inevitable argument over who rides in the front seat. A smart child care worker has a regular random selection process for just this kind of problem (odds and evens, tossing coins, drawing straws, etc.).

TAKING THE CHILDREN OUT

Before you set out, set the ground rules. You do not want the children acting inappropriately in the community. For one thing, it can give your facility a bad name. For another, being able to behave appropriately in public places is an important skill.

The ground rules depend, of course, on where you're going. Fights and violent arguments are always out. Cheering wildly is in for baseball games but out for church services. Courteous behavior toward the public is absolutely required. Residential facilities are easy targets for the public's anger, and it is not unknown for them to have been closed because the surrounding community did not want them. It's up to you to see that your facility has a good image.

Be sure that everyone is dressed suitably, depending on where you're going.

And, before you drive the kids anywhere, make sure that anyone who gets carsick is next to a window—a simple but obvious precaution.

By the way, when you are taking the kids out for a fun activity, *they* are the ones who should be having the fun. *You are at work.* Keep alert for dangerous behavior and don't let youngsters stray away from the group. Don't get so caught up in the activity that you forget to do your job.

INDOOR ACTIVITIES

A child care worker has to know some good indoor activities; they provide quick alternatives if an outdoor activity gets rained out. Indoor activities are also easy on the budget.

We won't say much about the standard board-and-card games. Children love them but usually need a staff member to act as umpire. One of the extra benefits of your job is becoming an expert on Monopoly rules.

There is no doubt that putting together a tournament, especially if the winners get a prize, adds spice to any game activity. This doesn't mean, however, that you *should* do it. Some groups of children cannot handle the added pressure of competing. Someone invariably gets angry and blows up. Don't start any heavy competition unless you know that the group can handle it.

Children love charades and other acting games. One worker tells of an activity that started with impersonations of various staff members. The children liked it so much that, with the worker's help, they built it into a play about the residence that they eventually performed for the whole facility on a Variety Night. He says, "I couldn't believe how closely the children had observed the various staff members, how well they knew their little mannerisms and tricks of speech. They also seemed to know that what they were doing could easily cease being funny and become hostile. They didn't let that happen."

Try the following in role-playing sessions:

- job interviews
- staff member and child (with child playing staff member and vice versa)
- principal and student
- teacher and student
- policeman and child (with staff member playing child)

To conduct a role-playing session, set up the ground rules at the beginning. There can, of course, be no actual violence. In situations in which violence is likely, a staff member should play the victim. You may find it best to join in the first role play to set the tone and get the ball rolling. Hold a discussion of each situation. You will find that children identify easily with authority figures and play them as harsh, violent, and rejecting.

Books on parlor games (you will find several good ones at the library) are good sources of interesting activities. There are also a good many books on various types of arts and crafts. Some require remarkable few materials. There are, for instance, several good books on making paper airplanes, making and flying kites, and simple magic tricks.

To get such activities started, organize the materials in advance. To involve the kids, the Tom Sawyer method is the best. Just sit down and start doing it yourself. Before you know it, you'll have all the help you need.

If you have a hobby like knitting, sewing, wood-work, or macrame, bring it in. By the way, some-times the quiet craft-type of activity can start meaningful conversations.

OUTDOOR SPORTS

We won't add much to the extensive literature available on outdoor athletic activities except to say that contact sports are out of the question unless you have expert supervision and the proper equipment. Softball, touch football, and basketball (indoor or outdoor) are favorites, but usually require a staff referee with an eagle eye and a will of iron. Less formal sessions of catch with a ball or Frisbee, or of shooting baskets, are also good. Some children and some staff members may enjoy running together. If you are a runner, you may find some kindred hardy souls who are up for a morning run.

Some facilities hold an occasional "Field Day" with track events interspersed with three-legged races, egg tosses, and so forth for the less athletic. This can be a lot of fun.

CAMPING

Camping with children can be fun but it is fraught with hazards. Planning ahead saves wear and tear on your nerves. First of all, pick a good time. Weekend camping trips near a large city are not a good idea. Campgrounds are crowded and noisy. During the summer, the middle of the week may be just as easy for you and will certainly be more pleasant.

Check your equipment carefully. Waterproof the tents and make sure all the gear works as it should.

Pick a location with plenty of activities, swimming, hiking trails, and so forth. The novelty of being in the country may soon wear off.

If you've got any ideas about really "roughing it," forget them unless you are an expert "tripper," in which case you don't need to read this anyway. Rough trips can be beautiful experiences for kids but such trips are dangerous and people have died as a result of lack of skill and knowledge. Canoe trips or other water activities are, in particular, extremely dangerous for the inexperienced. Never, under any circumstances, get into any small craft with children without an experienced hand *and* life jackets at all times. They won't like it, but they should not be given a choice.

Trail hazards can be fully as dangerous. Injury

or illness in the deep woods is obviously much more dangerous than it would be in a city. In some parts of the country, snakebite is a danger. A properly equipped medical kit *and* first-aid knowledge are musts if you go off the beaten track, as well as good woods skills, of course.

Before you take anyone anywhere, find out if any of the children have any medical problem or allergy, including an allergy to food or drugs, that might pose a problem. Bee-sting allergies are fairly common and can be fatal. If you have to get emergency medical help for a child, you must have the information the doctor will need. It's a good idea to carry a waterproof package with an emergency card on each child. This card should include a health summary, any special medical needs, a physical description, and contact numbers.

Most will prefer a less rugged style of "family camping" to more strenuous activity. It's the sort of thing that makes the real woodsperson sneer, but it's enjoyable. You drive right to the campsite fully equipped with a massive tent, stove, ice chest, recreational equipment, and dozens of odds and ends. If you're wise, you will outlaw radios, tape recorders, and other such noisemakers. They spoil any semblance of taking leave of civilization.

Children are fascinated by knives, hatchets, and axes. These items cause most of the accidents during camping. Children should not use these tools except under your supervision, and then only if you have taught them the proper methods. Keep your tools with you or locked in the car trunk at all times.

When time comes to bed down, you may discover something interesting. Most city kids are afraid of the dark. They actually may never have seen the real dark before. A child care worker tells us, "I remember my first trip. All the kids made elaborate beds of pine needles off away from the fire. However, as the night wore on, I found myself spending the night with six kids huddled around my sleeping bag. Every time the wind rustled the trees, someone would yell. I got very little sleep. The second night was better."

SWIMMING

Whatever the attractions of the old swimming hole, don't go swimming without a lifeguard. Don't, of course, swim in areas posted as dangerous.

In this, as in some other activities, you must avoid taking risks that you might take personally or with your own family. You must remember that, whether it is fair or not, the law is likely to hold you more responsible than it would the child's parents under similar circumstances. You're not expected to make mistakes or take chances, and if you do, you will not get the benefit of the doubt.

PETS

Sooner or later in your career, someone is going to suggest that your unit get a dog, cat, or other animal. Although a pet isn't really an activity, this is as good a place as any to talk about it.

Animals that live in residential facilities usually

have a hard time of it. Some children mistreat the animal. Others, out of ignorance, do things that confuse or irritate the pet. Staff will inevitably end up caring for it. You could, very wisely, decide that this is a bad idea from start to finish.

Cats are usually a completely bad idea. For some reason they are more apt to be abused. And then, there is a limit to what *any* cat will take before defending itself. Most people don't seem to know it but the common housecat can inflict extensive damage if sufficiently aroused.

Dogs, too, can be dangerous. The selection and training of the right dog to "work" at your facility (work is the right word) is a task for someone who knows dogs. Dogs, like people, have individual personalities; some dogs just don't like children. Rabbits, gerbils, and other highly vulnerable animals are not a good idea. Gold fish will be dead within a week. Snakes? Forget it!

On the other hand, children do love animals and can have very rewarding relationships with them. In our experience, having a dog at a facility works best if the dog belongs to one of the staff members, is completely good-natured, and is well trained. Under these circumstances, having a pet can work very well indeed.

8

Paperwork

C hild care paperwork usually falls into five categories:

- log entries
- reports on a particular child or children
- reports describing crises, accidents, illnesses, and other occurrences
- accounting for money
- time sheets and other strictly employment-related paperwork

This chapter deals mainly with the first three. Accounting and personnel practices are just too different from agency to agency for generalizations to be useful. You are well advised to find out about these matters, however.

Paperwork is part of your job. It's up to you to keep paperwork up-to-date. Unfortunately, child care people seem to regard paperwork as a form of torture devised by the administration to keep frontline workers from doing their jobs. Let's look at some of the reasons why this attitude is wrong.

Paperwork is the only way to coordinate the many people who work with a child. Written reports are valuable tools in planning future services for a child.

Much of child care paperwork is mandated by law or licensing regulation. A systematic failure to record the proper things can get your agency into trouble. Good reporting systems can offer protection against law suits, both for you and for the agency. Suppose, for example, that a parent alleges that you neglected a sick child, resulting in death or serious injury. You may have done all the right things but unless you have log entries and reports to back you up, you will probably be up the creek when a lawyer asks you, "Tell us precisely what you did on February 18th of last year?"

If none of these arguments impresses you, consider this: The person who signs your check considers paperwork a part of your job. If you neglect part of your job, pay raises and promotions aren't to be expected.

Many child care people, for some reason, do not feel comfortable expressing themselves in writing. Unfortunately, much child care paperwork involves a very difficult type of writing— description based on direct observation of a sequence of events, usually involving several people. As Ernest Hemingway once remarked, the hardest thing to write about is what actually happens.

A good child care worker has to be both a good witness and a competent writer. These skills can take years to perfect. The average person, as any policeman will tell you, is a poor witness. Our society, because it is predominantly large and urban, teaches us not to pay attention to others both out of fear of involvement and out of respect for privacy.

Try a pop quiz. What color are your best friend's eyes? What was he or she wearing the last time you met? Describe the person who served you the last time you went into a store to buy something. How tall is your next door neighbor? If you can answer all these questions reasonably accurately, you are an exceptional person. By the way, what *did* you do on February 18th of last year?

Unsnarling what happened in a fight or other crisis is even more difficult. In stressful situations, people frequently go blank or see and hear what they expect to see and hear rather than what actually happens.

Becoming a good reporter takes time and practice. Unfortunately, this is an area most child care training programs ignore. We hope that this situation will soon be corrected, but, in the meantime, you're on your own.

OBSERVATION

The most important form of observation is observation of day-to-day interactions in your unit. How do the children get along with each other? Which ones are friends? Who gets left out? How do children relate to different staff members? To an experienced child care worker, observation is second nature. It happens without conscious thought. But for the beginner, observation requires considerable effort.

One veteran remarks, "If I want to know what's going on in a unit, I find a central place—the living room, say—and I lie down on the couch and shut my eyes. For 10 minutes or so I just concentrate on listening to what the people in the room are doing and saying, and focusing on the noises from the rest of the house. I try to visualize what people are doing, what they're feeling. Then I get up and tour the facility, looking to see if I was right. First I concentrate on using my ears and then my eyes. I try to pick up the details, the little things that tell you what's going on." This sort of listening-and-looking exercise is very useful. It is well, of course, to let others know what you are doing, or else they may think your behavior a little strange. Eventually, with practice, you will develop an automatic sense of the unit and what's going on within it.

One of the most difficult forms of observation is observation of your own relationships. What we think other people think of us is usually obscured by what we want them to think of us. After all, how could any reasonable person be suspicious of or hostile toward such a thoroughly decent person?

One of the eternal truths of child care is that, if you want to be good, you have to take a good hard look at who you are and how you relate to people. What do you really want? To be loved? To be in control? To be a martyr? To be helpful? To make it to the end of the shift and go home? You can't really make good observations of your relationships until you know yourself. No book can help you there.

One thing that 10 years of child care will teach you is that you never really have anybody fooled. Human beings have a fine set of intuitions about each other. We aren't talking about magic. Whether you know it or not, you are constantly reading other people, watching their eyes and their bodies. You are even smelling them, without knowing it, and picking up clues about their emotional state. You can, indeed, smell fear, sexual attraction, and quite a number of other things. You just don't know that you can.

Learning to make use of these intuitive (perhaps some are instinctive) sources of information is part of becoming a good worker. But, like other sources of information, they are not to be accepted uncritically. You may indeed be picking up cues that the other person is giving off, but you also may be picking up your own biases. It is possible that the other person looks like someone from your past or comes from a background or race that makes you uncomfortable. No one can really teach you to understand nonverbal communication. There are a number of excellent books on the subject and through careful study you can begin to consciously read nonverbal cues.

How good an observer you are will finally depend on how willing you are to examine yourself and the world around you. Some workers get to the point at which they read the facility's environment like an Indian scout reading a trail. A very experienced worker once broke up a drug deal between two children because she saw one of them sitting on the porch after school. "He never does that," she said.

WRITING

Here is one of *our* biases and we might as well be honest about it. In our opinion, schools, and even universities, in recent years have done a poor job of teaching people to write.

Social service people write a strange variation of the English language that comes out sounding like German philosophy poorly translated by a computer programmer. A smokescreen of jargon utterly beclouds meaning. Plain English and ordinary sentence structure provide much more effective communication than jargon. Always use the simplest possible word to express an idea. Never use jargon if a more common word expresses the same thought. Get to the point in as few words as possible. An economical writer is loved by all. No one is likely to be impressed by length.

You will be using standard formats required by your agency for most written assignments. Make an outline of what you want to say before attempting any lengthy written report. Your old English teacher will be proud of you.

If you have difficulty writing, take a writing course. Such courses are usually offered by your local community college. Otherwise, get someone who writes well to read your reports and make comments. Try rewriting them until you feel good about the product.

LOG ENTRIES

Your agency will have its own format for using the log but we'll make some generalizations anyway. Log entries should always be dated and signed. It's difficult to find out who made a particular entry by analyzing the handwriting. Usually the time of the entry should be given and the approximate times of the events described should be given.

You will find that it's best to make an entry once every hour or so throughout your shift, whenever you get a moment of peace and quiet. This is much better than trying to remember everything at the end of the shift.

Your entry should be a brief summary of what happens in the unit. You should note when children leave, where they are going, when they are to return, and when they do return. (Sometimes, however, a separate sign-out sheet is used.) You should include a description of the activities within the unit.

Give details of any critical incident, any fight, any use of restraint, any suicide attempt or threat, and any other uncommon occurrence. Clearly state any condition or situation requiring action or observation by the next shifts, whether it be a leaky faucet or a fight brewing between two children.

Keep your log entries as brief as possible. Other staff members do not want to read about your thoughts and insights. The log is a working document; they want to know what they need to know on their shift. Meeting times are used for discussing the finer points. The log is also no place for telling other staff members things that you don't want to tell them to their faces. Nasty notes in the log irritate everyone.

Make sure that you follow agency policy concerning children reading the log. Some places allow it and others don't.

Never "cook the books." If something bad happens or if you make a mistake, log it honestly. Other staff members need to know what actually happened.

And one more thing. How is your handwriting? If it's anything but clearly readable, try printing. People do not want to spend all day trying to figure out whether you kissed, kidded, or killed Charlie.

Always end your log entries with a status report. Tell which children are in the unit, which ones out, and when the children who are out will return. In a sentence or two, summarize the mood of the unit. If your facility doesn't have a separate form or log for doing so, comment on each child's behavior and state of mind.

REPORTS ON CHILDREN

To repeat, start by outlining what you want to say and then write, adhering strictly to your outline.

A good child care report describes how the child behaves, how he or she relates with other children, how he or she relates with staff, and similar issues. It does *not* offer a psychiatric opinion or use labels like "paranoid," "schizophrenic," or "passive aggressive." You would *not* say: Charlie gave a passive-aggressive response when confronted with his behavior. Instead you might say: "When I told Charlie that I felt that he was trying to buy friendship from the other children by giving them things, he replied, 'I'm only doing what you staff told me to do.'" The first statement is a clinical interpretation and, in this case, possibly an incorrect one. The second statement is based on fact and direct observation.

You would not say: "Charlie has a negative self-image." You might say: "Charlie is continually downgrading himself and his own accomplishments. He frequently says, 'I can't do anything right.'" Facts and direct observations are what the child care worker brings to the treatment team.

A child may be a good source of information for the report. As a matter of fact, involving the child in the report may be useful for both of you. It offers you the opportunity to give him or her your thoughts and find out what the child thinks. You should, however, find out how your supervisor reacts to this idea *before* doing it. Some child care people just would not like the idea, although most would agree that nothing in your report should come as any surprise to the child.

When you are writing a report on a child, you should also consult other staff members to see what they think. As a report writer, it is your duty to seek and reflect the opinion of the child care staff. If you are the only person who gets along with the child, you should not be saying that the child "relates well to adults." You should, rather, examine why the child relates well to you and what the problem is in relating to others.

You should also refer to the child's file. The file is a collection of reports written by others on the child and family and may help you understand the child's current behavior.

INCIDENT REPORTS

Normally, any incident requiring the use of force, any serious fight, any suicide attempt, or any accident will require a report. Make sure that you know your agency's policies about this. Incident reports are usually also required whenever you take a child to a doctor. Minor medical problems handled in the unit are usually logged.

Incident reports are hard to write. A precise account of what happened is essential—who was involved, when it happened, where it happened, what actions were taken, and what the aftermath was. But after the kind of happening that requires such a report, it's often very hard to remember who hit whom first or what you did about it. The best thing to do is to sit down immediately and write out what you remember. If you aren't sure, say so. As you become more experienced, you will be able to give complete reports.

A child's running away usually requires a special report. Its basic purpose is to ensure that the police, the family, and everyone else who should be notified is notified. Documentation also usually ensures that the same people are notified promptly when the child returns. This report also describes the circumstances surrounding his or her running away and any efforts you have made to find the child. Most facilities have a form for this.

A number of other kinds of incidents should also be documented. If a child accuses you or another staff member of abuse, you should report the allegation to your supervisor in writing. This is the *only* sensible thing to do, no matter how ridiculous you may think the charge. This will, by the way, discourage anyone who considers making false charges.

9
Teamwork

As a child care worker you are part of a team of persons who work with the children. It's important that you work well with the other members of the team. Most facilities are like small worlds. You will get to know the other workers well. You will not always get along with them but you will have to find ways to work together. Sometimes you will feel that other professionals do not understand either you or your problems. Sometimes you will be right. As a child care worker, though, you can make a unique contribution to the treatment team.

Child care work will no doubt also bring you into contact with many other persons besides children and co-workers—the children's families, professionals, neighbors, community people, and so forth. Whether you know it or not, others will often judge your agency on the basis of your behavior. In contacts with others who are important in the children's lives, it's important that you be responsive and willing to work with them. You may sometimes come into contact with people who are violently opposed to your facility's presence in the community. By being courteous and willing to listen, you can help change their minds.

If you are like most workers, contact with children's families will be difficult; you will feel protective toward the children and not wish to see them upset. You may come to realize, however, that coming to terms with the family is a continuing, never-ending struggle for the child, for you, and for most of the human race. Your job is to help the children with their struggle, not keep them from it. Your job is to make the parents feel comfortable and involved.

You are responsible for your agency's image in the service community. This, in turn, influences the type of service the child receives. If, for example, you are slow to call the school to give them information they need, they may be slow to call you when the child is truant. If the police believe that your facility doesn't supervise children properly, they are less likely to view your missing-persons reports as particularly serious; they are also less likely to call you in immediately when they pick up one of your residents.

Finally, neighbors and other community residents must be considered. If community people feel that the facility does not respond to complaints promptly and fairly, they can get together a petition to have it closed. A number of small residences have been closed in this manner. Approached properly, the community is a resource. Approached improperly, it is a dangerous enemy.

FELLOW WORKERS

One child care worker remarks, "Working with these people is like being married to them. It's that close—but, you know, marriages usually have ways we can't use for resolving conflicts. No pillow talk, for one thing." That pretty well sums it up. After 10 years of child care, most of your good friends are persons you have worked with. Nobody else keeps the same hours.

Most groups of workers have at least some conflicts. Usually the frictions occur over precisely the sorts of issues that husbands and wives fight about: "You never clean up after yourself." "You're too hard (too easy) on the kids." "You undermine my authority." And so on.

Conflicts also frequently center on sex-role issues. Female workers complain about doing the housework while male workers play baseball. This particular complaint is usually completely justified. The solution, of course, is to share work equally.

While we're on the subject, let's take note of the fact that staff groups, like all groups of men and women, have sexual tensions. Child care work is, as well, a fairly intimate thing to do together. We should tell you that the consequences of involvement with someone else on staff can be serious. If it's love and you're really serious about each other, well, far be it from us to stand in the way. If it's just a casual involvement, you're in for trouble. A residential facility is no place to conduct such a relationship. It's bound to multiply existing tensions enormously. Experienced single workers tell us that they make it a rule never to date other workers. As for married workers, child care is hard enough on a marriage as it is.

Couples who work together can face some serious problems. One couple told us, "The real problem is that we're together *all* the time. We work together and spend our time-off together. We have to schedule time to be apart and stop driving each other crazy."

They also said, "The other people we work with have a hard time. Since we nearly always agree with each other, other workers are likely to feel overpowered and left out. We try not to talk about work when we are alone. That way, we have our differences in public and everybody feels better."

On most jobs, you can choose to ignore the people you don't get along with but a good child care team has to settle its differences. You can't do good child care with someone you don't respect. You don't have to agree on everything or be exactly alike but you do have to respect each other and you do have to communicate. The best way to do this is to talk out your differences openly. You may think it's unfair to ask you to deal with your personal opinions and feelings on the job but there's really no other way to build a good child care team.

One worker remembers a team he belonged to in which one of the male workers reminded all three of the female workers, in different ways, of their fathers. It took, he recalls, an entire month of intense discomfort and rather hostile interactions before this surfaced and was talked about. After talking about it, they were able to identify the male worker as a distinct and rather likable person. This team became a close-knit effective unit. He imagines that the tension would have persisted indefinitely if nothing had been done.

The fact is that working with children in a residential facility brings out all those suppressed feelings we have about our own families. The more homelike the residence, the more powerful the feelings. The very factors that make the facility a potentially powerful agent of positive change—the family-like environment—also make it a potential battleground. After all, most of us have powerfully negative as well as powerfully positive links to our past.

Another way of looking at it is that one of the unanticipated benefits of child care is the opportunity to work on your role as a member of a family group. Whatever role you play, as a father, mother, son, daughter, brother, or sister, will emerge and you will have to deal with it. Good supervisors realize that a staff group needs to talk out a wide range of issues, and offer the group guidance and a safe environment for doing so.

COMMUNICATION

Maintaining good communication is the primary problem for any staff group. Someone who has never worked in child care would probably be surprised to learn the sheer multitude of things child care staff members have to tell each other.

One of the most important values in child care is relatively consistent treatment of the children. A

staff member who makes a promise, sets a consequence, or makes arrangements may not be around
to carry through. The worker must be able to
count on other staff members who will be there. A
worker who make promises or arrangements without communicating them is going to be resented,
as is a worker who fails to carry through on
arrangements and promises.

In addition to messages regarding children,
there's plenty to communicate about in just running the household, handling money, keeping up
the stock of toilet paper and acne blemish cream,
making sure that every child has a good winter
coat, and so on. Housewives have been saying for
years that people just don't understand how hard
it is to keep a home going. Child care workers find
out just how true that is.

You have to keep alert, read the log, listen carefully, and, unless you have a photographic memory,
write details down. A personal memo book small
enough to fit into your pocket is a good idea. Write
down what you have to do and cross off each item
as you complete it.

SHARING THE WORK

Aside from missed communication, the major
friction in child care groups comes from feeling
that the detail work is not shared fairly. Good child
care workers sometimes feel that they are simply
too valuable to take care of details, that they
should spend all their time with the children.

If you ever start feeling this way, think again. Handing out the lunch money, cooking a meal, fixing a broken window, or doing any of the other mundane tasks that have to be done are powerful nonverbal statements of your commitment to the kids. Doing these kinds of things with and for kids is what makes the child care worker a powerful force in their lives.

As we suggested before, conflicts over work are frequently battles of the sexes. We have to support what female workers have to say about this. The notion that traditional divisions of work are somehow healthy for the children is absolute nonsense. Seeing adults who are able to work together in harmony is far more positive. Female workers should realize, though, that many men don't know how to do household tasks. Inability frequently masquerades as unwillingness. As well, men frequently just don't notice the little things that need doing; they have to be taught. This can be much more difficult and frustrating than doing it yourself, but it pays dividends.

PROFESSIONAL COURTESY

A third frequent cause of discord has also been mentioned here. There is nothing that causes resentment like showing up late to relieve a worker who has already put in a long shift and wants to go home. Showing up late for meetings is even worse; everyone is kept waiting. Be on time.

Common courtesy is very important. Child care workers work together so closely that it's awfully easy to stick your elbow into someone else's eye without meaning to. Good manners are an asset.

MEETINGS, MEETINGS, MEETINGS

Participation in a variety of meetings is an everyday fact of child care. Unfortunately, no one seems to provide training for this. If you don't hate meetings now, you soon will. People in the helping professions have a distressing tendency to talk too much. Most meetings are about twice as long as they need to be. Child care workers are among the worst offenders. After spending all day with children, it's very comfortable to find yourself in the company of adults.

Child care people talk about children. There's nothing wrong with that, except that at a meeting the story you are telling should have some kind of point and should be related to the agenda at hand. If it's after work and you're sitting down to have a few beers (or herbal teas, if you prefer), you can just swap yarns. *Not* at meetings. On the other hand, it's well to remember that child care meetings are not like business meetings. You can have an agenda and proceed through it in a businesslike fashion but it isn't good to become too much of a stickler for protocol. ("If it's not on the agenda, I won't talk about it!") After all, much of what goes on at meetings happens informally. If the only outcomes you allow are the ones you expect, you miss a good deal of the really creative ideas.

Generally, staff meetings have a secondary, usually unstated goal in addition to the primary goals. The staff meeting allows a good supervisor to check the temperature of the water and see how the staff members are feeling and interacting. The supervisor knows that this will have a lot to do with what kind of care the children are getting. If there is tension, it will come out at the meeting and can be dealt with. This isn't necessarily on the agenda.

Bearing all this in mind, we still favor a relatively business-like approach, somewhere in between sitting around telling stories and IBM. If you are to make a presentation, plan it in advance. Make notes or write out the whole thing if that's the best way for you. Keep it brief and try to offer the group your thoughts and recommendations for discussion and making decisions. If, for example, you're reporting on safety readiness, you should end your report by identifying weaknesses in the safety program and making suggestions for correcting them. This may sound like simple-minded advice but you will soon discover that a great many people don't follow it.

FAMILIES

Depending on your agency's policies, you may have either little or a lot of contact with children's families. In our opinion, however, relationships with children's families are vital. We're also of the opinion that the area of family involvement is the major weakness of both agencies and workers. The roots of the problem lie partly in the kind of people we are and our reasons for working in child care. Many workers find it easy to identify with and feel compassionate toward children. They may have little compassion for the parents because they hold the parents responsible for the children's problems.

Child care workers are often responsible for a major part of the day-to-day communication with parents. The worker is in a position to have a great deal of influence on the relationship between the facility and the family.

Parents usually feel guilty about out-of-home placement. They see child care staff members as the people who have taken over their parental responsibilities. They may resent you, idealize you, or do both at the same time. They are likely to feel embarrassed talking to you. They may see you as a witness to their shame. They may feel compelled to tell you the most intimate details of their lives or may seem unwilling to talk to you at all. One thing you may be sure of, however, they are watching you carefully and listening to you closely.

Parents will frequently perceive rejection in seemingly innocent remarks. You might, for example, call to arrange a visit and say something like, "You know, Mrs. Wilson, Ann's winter coat is a little old. We're thinking of getting a new one." Months later you may discover that Mrs. Wilson remembers this casual aside as a severe criticism of her ability to provide for her child. (But then again, maybe it was.)

Despite your best efforts there will be parents, as there will be children, with whom you cannot form positive relationships. One child care worker remarks, "I think the child care literature about families is contributing to a myth. We have started to feel that we, as people, must always be able to form positive relationships with these parents. Don't get me wrong; I can respect, even like, most parents. Most are amazingly strong and have held together through stuff I know I couldn't take. But I think we have to recognize that we aren't saints. Then, when we run into someone we can't stand, maybe we'll let someone else handle it."

This worker's point is well taken. Good family work does not consist of pretending to like people, or of overlooking the destructive things some parents have done and may continue to do to their children. In some cases, a worker's biases—or values—can be strong enough to make turning the family over to another worker the best move.

The essence of the matter is, of course, that learning and growth are painful processes. Children are not placed in residential facilities for cold storage. One of the primary goals of care is assisting the family to find new patterns of interaction. The residence offers a respite for both child and family and the possibility, with the help of others, to try out new behaviors. The ultimate end—the decision whether child and family can be reunited or to make another plan—is being shaped by what happens every day.

Feelings About Placement

How do families feel about their child being placed in a residential facility? Most feel guilty, resentful, and at least a little relieved. The guilt is

intense. Failure as a parent is a serious matter in
our culture. Friends, neighbors, and relatives are
unlikely to be sympathetic and may be downright
hostile. Guilt quickly turns into resentment. The
parents may be angry with the child, with the facility, and with the placing agency—with all the people involved in what the parents may see as a humiliating experience. As for relief, the kinds of
children who are placed in residential facilities are
rarely easy to live with. It is a relief to know that if
the child is picked up by the police, skips school,
or runs away, it will be someone else's problem.
Frequently, this sense of relief only intensifies the
guilt.

Parents' reactions to their own feelings vary.
Some parents get openly hostile. Others idealize
the facility and staff, abdicating all immediate
responsibility for the child. ("My child is so bad
that ordinary people like me can't take care of him.
It takes special people like you.") This, of course,
relieves the parents' sense of having failed. Some
parents ally themselves with the child against
the "authorities." They may "spoil" the child, hide
his or her delinquencies when on home visits, or
make extravagant promises that cannot be kept.
They may avoid contact altogether.

Most parents are confused and hurt about the
placement. Most really do want to do the right
thing for the child and respond immediately to
helpful, supportive gestures.

Your Role

As a child care worker, you may not carry primary responsibility for working with parents. You

will probably, however, have more direct contact with them than anyone else. When they call or visit, they will probably talk to you. When visits are arranged or any of the other routine contacts are made, you will probably be responsible. When parents and child talk about the agency, it is likely to be you, not the social worker or the administrator, who is discussed. You are just more visible and more readily available.

You are also the person who takes over what are normally regarded as parental responsibilities. From the parent's point of view this makes you a key person. The parent may or may not understand what treatment staff members do or what a social worker is, but they certainly do understand that you are responsible for the child's general well-being—for food, clothing, and all the rest of it.

You should not try to be a family counselor. You can listen supportively to anything parents wish to say to you but don't start making too many suggestions about what the parents should do. Family counseling is complex and takes a great deal of training and practice.

Never make any promises that you are not empowered to make. Check everything out with your supervisor and other team members. When parents call to ask if their child may visit or be visited on the following weekend, you may be tempted to say, "Sure, I don't see any reason why not." If it turns out that there is a good reason why not, the parents will feel betrayed and angry.

If the parents ask a question you cannot answer, check it out or refer them to the appropriate person. If the parents tell you about a serious personal or family problem, refer them to a professional. One of your functions, as a member of the treatment team, is to act as a liaison between clients and professionals. If the parent needs a service offered by a professional on your team, speak to the professional and hook them up. Offer moral support if the parent is fearful about "seeing a psychologist."

When parents visit, treat them like welcome guests. This may sound silly, but don't forget to offer them tea or coffee. This is a very meaningful gesture in our culture and will serve to make parents much more comfortable.

Parents need to see where their child is living. If they have not seen the facility, take them on a tour with their child. Show them the child's hobbies or projects and take time to tell them how the child is doing.

Hassles with parents about clothing are common. It may be one way parents express their continuing interest in the children's lives. These hassles usually occur because a piece of clothing the parents gave the child has been lost, stolen, or traded, or because the family does not like the way the child is dressing. This is one good reason to carefully monitor children's clothing.

Whenever parents do make a critical remark about the facility's care of the child, don't get defensive. Try to reply in a manner that recognizes the parents' right to express a continuing interest in their child's welfare.

Many of your contacts with parents will consist of making arrangements for visits. The worst thing that you can do is forget to communicate these

arrangements. This might result in the child showing up at home unannounced, the parents arriving
at the facility unexpectedly, or the child looking
forward to a visit that will not occur. Make sure to
write down all arrangements, enter them in the
log, and communicate them verbally to the child
and other staff members. Take no chances.

There are some agencies in which parents are
essentially the responsibility of someone else, such
as the social worker or administrator. No matter
how you may feel about this procedure, do not fail
to communicate your observations to them. Your
anger may indeed hamper their performance of
their jobs, but the ultimate victim of your failure to
communicate your feelings will be the child, not
the staff person.

SCHOOLS

It's important that you work closely with teachers and school personnel and make an effort to
understand their problems. You will soon notice
that children who may be easy to handle in the
facility may be constantly in trouble at school. You
may be tempted to believe that this is because you
know how to handle them but the teachers don't.
You will probably be wrong.

Most of the children have school problems. For
many, school consistently has been an experience
of failure. Some children *do* behave very differently at school. A person who spent years in child
care before becoming a teacher remarks: "I teach
a class for the same kind of children I once worked
with at a residential school setting. I remember

thinking that the teachers didn't know how to manage children. Well, children usually like child care workers but many hate teachers and have a very hard time being in school. The view looks very different from here."

What teachers want most of all is your support for their expectations. This means making sure that the children do their homework and come to school properly prepared. Make sure that you keep the school informed of any child's absence. Handle promptly any paperwork the school sends home. Give prompt attention to any request. If the school calls and asks you to come get a child, do so immediately. It's nearly always best to get the child out, let things cool off, and go back for a meeting.

Do not discuss confidential information about the child or family with school personnel. Although this may seem to be a good way to get them to go easy on a troubled child, it's also a breach of confidentiality.

POLICE

Child care people do not generally like dealing with the police. Most feel that the police are unduly harsh and just don't understand children's problems. But if you work in an open, community-based setting, you will probably have to deal with the police and it will be important to maintain good relationships. Actually, the police aren't much different from anyone else. Most are reasonable persons trying to do an unreasonable job.

Most often, your contacts with the police will involve making a missing-persons report, which we discussed previously in detail. Try to have the information ready when the police get there. And when a child returns, call the police *immediately* to cancel the report.

Conclusion

We hope that you have enjoyed and benefited from this book. As you have seen, child care work, on its most fundamental level, consists of many everyday elements. Viewed as a whole, however, child care work may be described as a challenging field that is gradually gaining broad recognition as a professional discipline. Some colleges and universities, for example, now are giving academic credit to persons previously or at present involved in the child care field. This trend is likely to continue and become more widespread.

But child care work is rewarding also on an even more important level because it represents responsible and committed people caring for others in a very practical and human way. Since child care is direct care, it is an expression of love, a demonstration of humanity, and a respected discipline.

We wish you continued growth as a child care worker.

The Author

Jesse E. Crone is Executive Director of Baptist Children's Services of Pennsylvania, New Jersey, and Delaware, where he has had a long and extensive association with child care and social service. Since 1966, he has developed numerous social service and child-oriented programs. He has taught psychology, participated in the programs of various mental health clinics, and lectured at Eastern College and the University of Pennsylvania. He is also the author of *Creative Change in a Caring Agency*, the history of a representative child care facility.

Mr. Crone's activities have brought him close to child care work and child care workers.